The Culture Book

Fiona MacDonald
Antony Mason

Miles Kelly

PUBLISHING

First published in 2003 by
Miles Kelly Publishing Ltd
The Bardfield Centre
Great Bardfield
Essex CM7 4SL

Copyright © Miles Kelly Publishing 2003

2 4 6 8 10 9 7 5 3 1

Authors
Fiona MacDonald, Antony Mason

Design
Starry Dog Books

Project Editor
Belinda Gallagher

Editorial Assistant
Lisa Clayden

Artwork Commissioning
Lesley Cartlidge

Indexer
Jane Parker

Picture Research
Ruth Boardman, Liberty Newton

Colour Reproduction
DPI Colour, Saffron Walden, Essex

ISBN 1-84236-273-9

Printed in Singapore

British Library Cataloguing-in-Publication Data
A catalogue record for this book is available from the British Library

www.mileskelly.net
info@mileskelly.net

Contents

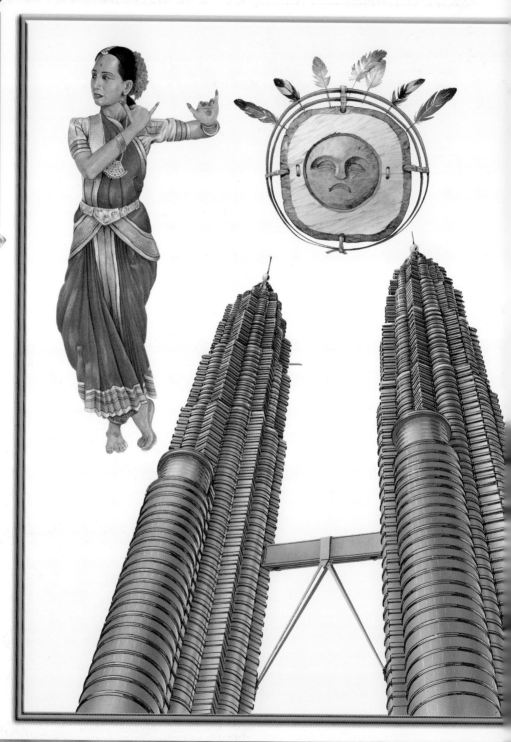

Introduction

The word 'culture' is traditionally used to describe different art forms such as music, dance, literature and drama. But culture isn't just about art and opera. It's about the way people live, their lifestyles and behaviour. The following pages reveal a world steeped in culture. As well as discovering the beauty of ballet, the richness of music, amazing architecture and powerful drama, you can read about the importance of stories and traditions passed down from generation to generation, education, celebrations and political ideas. This book will help you trace the history of culture and its influence on modern-day life.

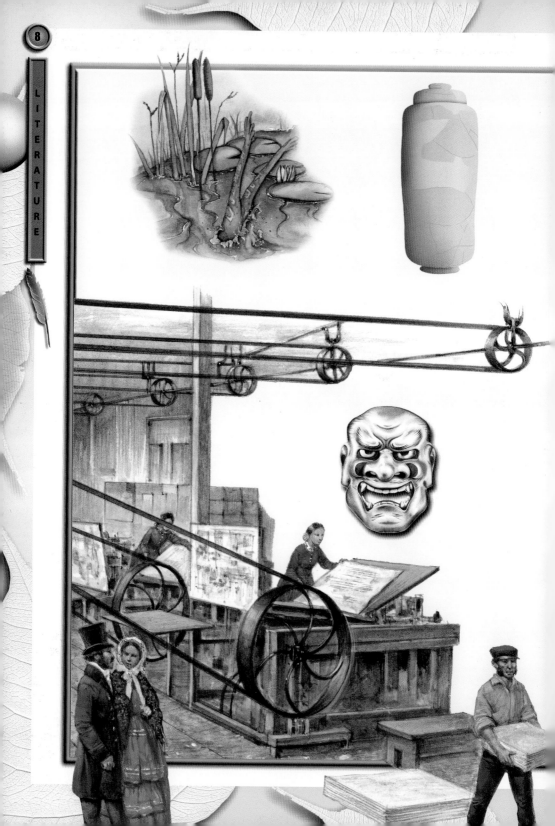

Literature

THE history of civilization dates back to just over 5000 years ago, about the same time that writing began. This is no coincidence: Writing has played a key part in the development of civilization and culture. It was used to keep records about rulers and their people – their history, religion, deeds, and laws. But it was also a way of preserving stories and ideas. Through writing, we know about myths and legends of ancient times and what ancient peoples such as the Romans did and thought, and what their imaginations produced. Writers have been adding their own contributions to literature ever since, demonstrating the extraordinary inventiveness of the human mind in stories, novels, poetry and plays.

LITERATURE

Epics and sagas

STORIES were told for thousands of years before they were written down. They were told from memory, and then passed from one generation to the next by word of mouth. Some of the earliest stories were epics – long tales in poetry that recounted the adventures of great heroes in the mythical past. To hold an audience's attention, epics had to be full of exciting events, romance, strong characters, wisdom, humour, and suspense. The long medieval tales of adventure from Norway and Iceland were called sagas.

◩ JONGLEURS AND MINSTRELS

In medieval Europe, *jongleurs* ('jugglers') put on shows in market fairs that combined juggling, acrobatics, music and poetry. They also created epic tales about knights, love and war. Minstrels entertained the rich and powerful in their castles.

◩ KING ARTHUR

Ancient legends from Britain and France tell of King Arthur and his knights. These tales of heroic deeds, love and Christian values are not just exciting stories. They also reveal how medieval knights thought they should behave according to the codes of chivalry. In the tale of King Arthur's death, his sword Excalibur is magically raised from the lake into which it has been thrown.

◪ VIKING SAGAS

The Vikings of Scandinavia and Iceland told sagas— long, exciting tales of warriors that mixed legend with true history. The sagas were created by poets called *skalds*, who made a living by telling the tales as entertainment. The sagas were not written down until long after Viking times.

◪ DANTE

The *Divine Comedy* is an epic poem of more than 14,000 lines, written by the Italian poet Dante Alighieri (1265–1321). It tells of a journey by Dante and two escorts (first the poet Virgil, then Beatrice) down to hell and up to heaven.

◪ HEROIC ADVENTURE

The epic poem *Beowulf* dates from about AD 750 and is based on Scandinavian folk tales. The hero Beowulf rids the Danes of a water monster called Grendel, and his hook-fingered mother. He becomes king, but dies killing a dragon.

THE TROJAN HORSE

Homer's great epic, the Iliad, *tells of the 10-year war between Greece and the city of Troy. According to legend, the Greek soldiers finally tricked their way into Troy by hiding inside a giant wooden horse, left, as a gift for the Trojans. Once inside the city, they opened Troy's gates to the Greek armies.*

◪ THE ARABIAN NIGHTS

Scheherazade, so the story goes, was the wife of a murderous Arab king, who kept herself alive by telling him riveting, magical stories. Many of them are very famous, such as the tales of Aladdin, Ali Baba and Sinbad the Sailor. These Arab folk tales are all at least 1000 years old.

◪ THE *ODYSSEY*

One of the world's most famous epics is the *Odyssey*. It was created in ancient Greece in about 700 BC, perhaps by a poet called Homer (no one is sure). It recounts the adventures of Odysseus on his 10-year journey home after the war against Troy. In one tragic scene, Odysseus's faithful old dog Argus dies as his master reaches his home town.

The written word

BEFORE writing was invented, all information had to be remembered and communicated as spoken words. But once writing developed, it could be stored and sent from one place to another. The Mesopotamians in the Middle East were among the first people to develop writing, in about 3400 BC. To start with, writing was used for lists, such as orders for goods sent by merchants. But soon people were writing letters, history and stories. This was the beginning of literature. The word 'literature' comes from the Latin *litteratura*, meaning writing.

◩ PICTURE-WRITING

The ancient Egyptians invented a system of writing that used more than 800 picture symbols. It was called hieroglyphics, or 'sacred carving', because it was used to write religious texts on temple walls.

◤ THE ROSETTA STONE

For centuries, Egyptian hieroglyphics were a mystery. But in 1799 a stone was found near Rosetta, in Egypt, inscribed in Egyptian, Greek, and hieroglyphics. By comparing them, scholars were able to work out what the hieroglyphics meant.

◪ ROMAN SCRIPT

Our alphabet is based on the Roman alphabet, which in turn came from the Greek alphabet. The Romans wrote in Latin, in capital letters. Latin became the language of the Christian church. Small 'lower-case' letters were invented in medieval times, as seen in this handwritten French book from the 13th century.

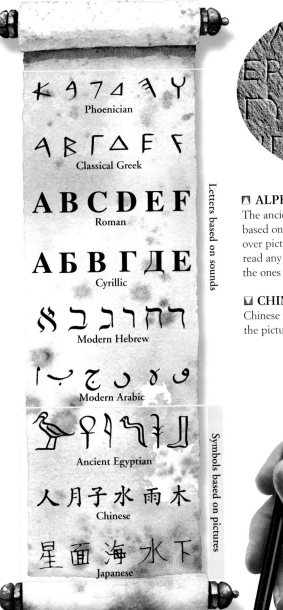

Phoenician

Classical Greek

Roman

Cyrillic

Modern Hebrew

Modern Arabic

Ancient Egyptian

Chinese

Japanese

Letters based on sounds

Symbols based on pictures

◪ ALPHABET OF SOUNDS

The ancient Greeks used a system of writing based on sounds, not pictures. The advantage over picture-writing was that you could write and read any word with a set of just 24 letters, like the ones on this ancient Greek tombstone.

◪ CHINESE CHARACTERS

Chinese writing is based on pictures. Over time, the pictures became stylized into symbols, known as 'characters'. There are about 1000 basic Chinese characters, which represent a word or idea. The characters can be understood by peoples who speak different languages – they recognize the character, but pronounce it differently.

◪ LETTERS AND CHARACTERS

Sound-based alphabets can be traced back to the Phoenicians, who lived in Lebanon in ancient times. Japanese writing is based on the Chinese system, the oldest form of writing in use today.

Sacred writing

SOME of the greatest works of early literature were stories about the gods. The stories were often interwoven with historical facts. Originally they were not written down, but were passed by word of mouth from one generation to the next. The great Hindu epic the *Mahabharata* – all 220,000 lines of it – was passed down as a spoken work for over 2000 years before it was printed for the first time in the 19th century. Such sacred works are often celebrated not just for what they say, but also for the beauty and poetry of their language.

◩ HOLY BOOK OF ISLAM

Muslims believe that the Qu'ran, the holy book of Islam, contains the actual words of God as revealed to Mohammed, the prophet of Islam, after about AD 610. For this reason it is treated with great respect. Scribes copying the Qu'ran use especially beautiful forms of Arabic writing.

◪ HANDWRITTEN SCROLLS

The Jews believe that God revealed his laws to Moses on Mount Sinai, perhaps about 1200 BC. These laws form the holy book called the *Torah*, still kept in the form of large, handwritten scrolls (shown here being carried). The *Torah* is the same as the first five books of the Bible, but in a wider sense the term also covers all Jewish scriptures, laws and customs.

◩ THE DIAMOND SUTRA

The world's earliest-known printed book is a copy of the *Diamond Sutra*, a sacred Buddhist text about the perfection of wisdom, which 'cuts like a diamond'. It was printed in China in AD 868. Each page was printed from a carved woodblock, and glued together as a scroll.

DAVID AND GOLIATH

The Old Testament of the Bible contains a mixture of Jewish history, laws, teachings and folklore. One of its famous stories tells how the boy David (later a great king) bravely took on the giant Philistine warrior Goliath and killed him with a well-aimed slingshot.

◪ SAINT PAUL

When it started, Christianity was a Jewish movement. Saint Paul preached its message to non-Jews across the Roman Empire. His teaching is preserved in the Bible as a collection of letters, called Epistles, to the new Christian communities.

◪ SCRIPTURE OF THE SIKHS

The main scripture of the Sikhs is called *Adi Granth*, or 'First Book', a collection of nearly 6000 hymns of the Sikh gurus, or religious teachers. They were written down between 1604 and 1704. The book is also known as *Guru Granth Sahib*, because it is treated as if it were a living guru.

THE DEAD SEA SCROLLS

The Bible was preserved through the ages in handwritten copies. In 1947, 2000-year-old scrolls of the Old Testament books were found near the Dead Sea in Israel, stored in pots. They are much older than other known copies.

The printing revolution

UNTIL about 600 years ago there were very few books, and they were expensive. Almost all books in Europe were written by hand, each one taking months to produce. Only educated and rich people used them. But in about 1438, Johannes Gutenberg invented an efficient way of printing, using 'movable type'. Suddenly it was possible to mass-produce books in large numbers, and quite cheaply. More people began to read, and soon newspapers, pamphlets and posters were being printed, too.

◗ WOODBLOCK PRINTING

In woodblock printing, which dates back to 9th-century-AD China, each page is separately carved. The Japanese continued to use this method, as seen in this print of about 1850.

◖ THE PRINTING INDUSTRY

By 1850, in Europe and the United States, large printing workshops – like this one in Boston – were printing and assembling thousands of copies of illustrated books and magazines in just a few days. The new steam-powered rotary presses, introduced in 1846, could print 8000 sheets an hour.

◪ HERBERT INGRAM

The first magazine to use lots of pictures was the *Illustrated London News*, founded as a 'weekly' by Herbert Ingram in 1842. The pictures were printed from engravings on metal plates. After the 1880s, photographs were used.

NEWSPAPER PRINTING

Newspapers today are printed on machines called web presses. Paper is fed from huge rolls through the press at a rate of up to 1000 metres a minute. The pages are then folded and cut, ready for distribution.

GUTENBERG

In about 1438, the German Johannes Gutenberg developed a way of printing using 'movable type'. First he cast hundreds of individual metal letters in moulds. Then he arranged these letters into pages of text, which he printed on a press – a far quicker method than woodblock printing.

PROPAGANDA

Printing is a good way of spreading information. Millions of copies of a document can be made quickly. Of course, the information may be true or false. Governments print 'propaganda'– pro-government literature – to win support, such as this poster produced by the Chinese Communists when they came to power at the end of a civil war in 1949.

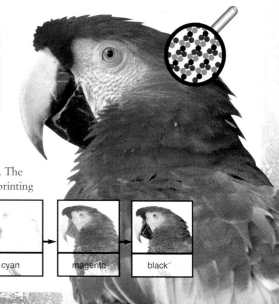

COLOUR PRINTING

If you look at a printed colour picture under a magnifying glass, you will see a mass of tiny dots. The colour is actually made up of just four different printing inks: yellow, cyan (blue), magenta (red) and black. Each colour is applied by a separate roller as the paper passes through the printing press.

yellow → cyan → magenta → black

The novel: Early classics

DURING the 15th century, collections of stories, such as Boccaccio's *Decameron*, became popular in Europe. The collections were called 'novels', from the Italian word *novella*, meaning a piece of news or a tale. By 1605 the novel had developed into a long, imaginary tale with one or more central characters, but it was not until the 18th century that the novel became a popular form of entertainment. As more people learned to read, printing increased and readers were able buy their own copies of imaginary worlds.

◤ PRINCE GENJI

The Tale of Genji is thought to be the world's oldest full-length novel. It was written about AD 1000 by Murasaki Shikibu, a lady-in-waiting to the empress of Japan. It tells the story of Prince Genji and his various loves.

◀ DOSTOEVSKY

Russia has produced some of the world's greatest novelists. Feodor Dostoevsky (1821–81) is famous for novels such as *Crime and Punishment*, *The Idiot* and *The Brothers Karamazov*. Although they deal with serious subjects such as prisons, madness and murder, they also sparkle with humour and a sense of the absurd, and contain brilliantly drawn characters. Dostoevsky had a major influence on the development of modern literature.

DEFOE AND SELKIRK

Daniel Defoe's Robinson Crusoe *was based on the story of a real-life castaway. In 1704 a Scottish sailor named Alexander Selkirk (left) was stranded on an island off Chile. Five years passed before he was rescued.*

◤ CHARLES DICKENS – COMIC GENIUS

The novels of Charles Dickens (1812–70) were hugely popular. Set in the industrial world of Victorian England, they are filled with larger-than-life characters. In *A Christmas Carol*, the miserly Scrooge is haunted by ghosts who reveal to him the damaging effects of his meanness.

◪ TOM SAWYER

Some characters from novels have become world famous. *The Adventures of Tom Sawyer*, by American author Mark Twain (1835–1910), tells the story of a mischievous but engaging boy growing up in Missouri, USA. Numerous film versions have been made, including this one from 1938.

◪ JANE AUSTEN

Novels do not have to tell of great events or adventures. Jane Austen (1775–1817) was a genius at portraying the lives of ordinary people in a carefully observed way and with wry humor. Her novels include *Sense and Sensibility, Emma* and *Pride and Prejudice*.

◪ DON QUIXOTE, GALLANT HERO

When the first part of *Don Quixote de la Mancha* was published in 1605, it was an immediate bestseller. It is often said to be the first 'modern' novel. Written by the Spanish author Miguel de Cervantes (1547–1616), it follows the adventures of Don Quixote, an aging gentleman who mistakenly believes he is a knight living in the Age of Chivalry.

THE HUNCHBACK OF NOTRE DAME

Victor Hugo (1802–85) was one of the most famous of all French writers, celebrated for his poems and many novels. Perhaps his most famous novel is The Hunchback of Notre Dame, *in which he shows humans to be a blend of good and evil. The hunchback is Quasimodo, an outcast in the cathedral bell tower, who is shown kindness only by the woman he is sent to capture.*

The novel: Traditions

DURING the 19th century, writers began to explore the storytelling possibilities of the novel. They learned to combine intriguing characters with inventive plots, and used their imaginary worlds to make comments on the real world around them. Various types of novel developed, such as history novels, thrillers, detective novels and romantic novels. Novels have remained one of the most popular forms of literature ever since. They have been translated into numerous languages, and many of them are made into films.

◢ SCHINDLER'S ARK
Some novels are closely based on historical fact, like this novel by the Australian writer Thomas Keneally (born 1935). It tells the story of Oskar Schindler, a German who saved more than 1300 Jews from certain death in Nazi camps in Poland.

◢ WAR AND PEACE
Count Leo Tolstoy (1829–1910) was one of the greatest Russian novelists, as well as a playwright and philosopher who developed his own form of Christianity. He is most famous for his epic novel *War and Peace*. Set against the war with France under Napoleon (this scene is from the 1956 film version), it explains Tolstoy's view that history is chaotic and has no pattern.

DETECTIVE NOVELS
'The Murders in the Rue Morgue' by the American writer Edgar Allan Poe (1809–49) was probably the first detective story – one of the most popular forms of fiction. The most famous detective, often mistaken for a real person, was Sherlock Holmes, created by the British writer Arthur Conan Doyle (1859–1930).

◪ GARCÍA MÁRQUEZ

In the 1940s, a new kind of writing emerged from Latin America. Called 'magic realism', it mixed reality with imaginative fantasy.

One of the best-known books in this style is *One Hundred Years of Solitude* by the Colombian writer Gabriel García Márquez (born 1928). In 1982 he won the Nobel Prize for Literature.

◪ THE BRONTË SISTERS

The three Brontë sisters, Charlotte, Emily, and Anne, wrote some of the greatest novels of early Victorian England, and were a major influence on later novel writing. Much of their work is about human relationships and the powerful forces of love. Charlotte (1816–55) is most famous for *Jane Eyre* (shown here); Emily (1818–48) for *Wuthering Heights*; and Anne (1820–49) for *The Tenant of Wildfell Hall*.

◪ SALMAN RUSHDIE

Novels can contain ideas so strong that they provoke anger and fear. After the British novelist Salman Rushdie (born 1947) published *The Satanic Verses* in 1988, it was condemned as blasphemous (offensive to God) by the Muslim religious authorities in Iran. He has lived under the threat of assassination by religious fanatics ever since.

◪ JAMES BOND

One of the world's best-known fictional characters is James Bond, the secret service agent at the centre of a series of spy thrillers by the British novelist Ian Fleming (1908–64). All twelve of Fleming's Bond novels were made into films, five of them starring Sean Connery (shown here).

Poetry: Different kinds

SOME poems are very long, some very short. Some tell long and complicated stories, like the great epics of Homer. Others paint pictures of a brief moment. In some poems all the lines rhyme; others have no rhyming lines at all. In fact, it is not easy to say what poetry is exactly. But most poetry is written out in lines, while novels and short stories are written in continuous text, or 'prose'. Poetry also tends to use language inventively. The poet brings together language and ideas to say something new and memorable about the world.

🔲 JAPANESE HAIKU

The Japanese developed a very short type of non-rhyming poem called a haiku, usually just 17 syllables long, written as three lines (divided as 5-7-5 syllables). The aim was to capture a moment of intense perception, often linking a detail of nature with a sense of eternity. Here is an example from the poet Bashō (1644–94), a master of haiku:

Furuike ya, kawazu tobikomu, mizu no oto.

> *Breaking the silence*
> *Of an ancient pond,*
> *A frog jumped into*
> *water – a deep*
> *resonance.*

🔲 POETIC TALES

Geoffrey Chaucer (*c.*1345–1400) was the first great poet to write in English. His most famous work is *The Canterbury Tales*, a collection of 23 stories in verse told by a group of characters as they travel to Canterbury. Dramatic, romantic, touching, hilarious – together they paint a vivid picture of life in 14th-century England.

🔲 BALLADS

Originally ballads were popular songs written to accompany a dance. As poems, they usually tell a dramatic story using strong rhythm and rhyme. In the 15th and 16th centuries, many ballads were written about the legendary outlaw of Sherwood Forest, Robin Hood, and his band of men.

◻ POEMS OF LOVE AND LIBERTY

The French poet and novelist Victor Hugo (1802–1885) is best rememberd by the French for his poetry. His expressive use of language clearly portrayed his belief in liberty and his understanding of human suffering. Hugo was also a great romantic poet and this was firmly established by the publication of *The Orientals* in 1829.

CHILDREN'S POETRY

Young children love the musical sound of poetry. British writer A. A. Milne (1882–1956) – famous as the author of the stories about the bear Winnie-the-Pooh – wrote numerous funny poems for children. His two famous collections are: When We Were Very Young *and* Now We Are Six.

◻ THE ROMANTIC VIEW OF NATURE

In the late 18th century, a group of British poets gathered in the beautiful Lake District of northwest England and wrote about their feelings for nature. William Wordsworth (1770–1850), Robert Southey (1774–1843), and Samuel Taylor Coleridge became known as the 'Lake Poets'. They had a major influence on the way people looked at nature.

◻ POWERFUL IMAGES

Through the intensity of their language, poems are able to convey strong images of an imaginary world to the reader. In his famous long poem *The Rime of the Ancient Mariner*, the British poet Samuel Taylor Coleridge (1772–1834) paints a vivid picture of despair on board a ship cursed with bad luck after the mariner shoots an albatross, a seabird.

LITERATURE

Poetry: Poetic heroes

BECAUSE of the original way they see and describe the world, poets have held a special place in society since ancient times. Often in the past, they had an important influence on the way people viewed the world. Poets are concerned to capture in words people's feelings about all kinds of subjects – from love and death, to feelings about their country, or nature, or just the small things in everyday life. Or they might convey a powerful vision of a spiritual world beyond our daily lives. Some of the most successful poets became superstars in their day, and are celebrated as national heroes.

◪ HEAVEN AND HELL

The English poet John Milton (1608–74) wrote numerous poems, as well as pamphlets about the church and government. In the 1650s he went blind and had to dictate his work, including his great epic *Paradise Lost*. This tells how the angel Satan rebelled against God, who threw him out of Heaven.

GARCÍA LORCA

Writing with an intense feeling for his country, Federico García Lorca (1898–1938) became the best-known poet of his day in Spain. His poems often explore the theme of violent death. Lorca himself was shot by nationalist soldiers just before the outbreak of the Spanish Civil War.

◪ LORD BYRON

The English aristocrat George Gordon, Lord Byron (1788–1824), lived and died the life of a heroic Romantic poet. He became a celebrity across Europe after the publication of his long narrative poem *Childe Harold's Pilgrimage*. Byron died of fever while fighting to liberate the Greeks from Turkish rule.

'SEASON OF MISTS...'

John Keats (1795–1821) is one of the greatest English poets, celebrated for his rich imagery. He wrote both narrative verse and 'lyric' poems such as odes, which are short and expressive of feelings or sensations. Autumn, for example, he describes as a 'season of mists and mellow fruitfulness...'. Keats died of tuberculosis, aged just 25.

MARINA TSVETAYEVA

Marina Tsvetayeva (1892–1941) was one of Russia's greatest poets of the 20th century. She opposed the Communist Revolution of 1917 and left Russia in 1922, but still wrote lovingly of her homeland. She returned in 1939, but was forced to leave Moscow during World War II. Lonely and isolated, she committed suicide.

ELIZABETH BARRETT BROWNING

In 1844, *Poems* made Elizabeth Barrett (1806–61) one of the best-known poets in England. She married the poet Robert Browning (1812–89), and they lived mainly in Italy. She was celebrated for her love poems, and her outspoken opinions about politics, slavery and women in society.

YEVGENY ONEGIN

Aleksandr Sergeyevich Pushkin (1799–1837) is Russia's most celebrated and beloved poet, and is known as the founder of Russian literature. His greatest work, *Yevgeny Onegin*, is a novel in verse. It was made into an opera by the Russian composer Tchaikovsky (a set from the opera is shown here). Pushkin died age 37 after fighting a duel.

Drama

PLAYWRITING is one of the oldest forms of literature. Plays written 2500 years ago by the ancient Greek dramatist Aeschylus are still performed today. The greatest plays capture the imagination of the spectators and can make them sit on the edge of their seats with fear or excitement, or cry with laughter or emotion. But a good play depends on more than just the written words – it needs good actors to interpret them and scenery, costumes and lighting to add to the drama.

◣ CLASSICAL THEATRE

In ancient times plays were a hugely popular form of entertainment. In Europe the tradition began in Greece, and was later adopted by the Romans. Open-air theaters such as this Roman theater at Jarash in Jordan held as many as 15,000 people.

◣ FAUST

The greatest figure in German literature is Johann Wolfgang von Goethe (1749–1832), poet, playwright and scientist. One of his most famous works is the two-part drama *Faust*, which tells the story of a scholar who sells his soul to the devil (seen here in a 1926 film version).

◤ A NEW KIND OF PLAY

The Russian playwright Anton Chekhov (1860–1904) helped to shape modern drama. He was more interested in exploring the interaction of his characters' thoughts and emotions than in devising an eventful plot. This scene is from a film version of *The Three Sisters*.

🔲 *NŌ* DRAMA

Japanese *Nō* drama dates
back to the 14th century. Male
actors, often in masks like this one,
chant the words and dance to music in
a highly stylized performance, which has been
fixed by hundreds of years of tradition. *Nō*
theatre was intended for aristocratic audiences,
while another form of traditional Japanese
theatre, *Kabuki*, was for ordinary people.

🔲 SHAKESPEARE

One of the most
celebrated writers
ever is the English
playwright and poet
William Shakespeare (1564–1616). He wrote
some 37 plays, including many of the classics of
theatre, such as the tragedies *Othello, Macbeth*
and *Romeo and Juliet* and the comedy
A Midsummer Night's Dream. The huge success
of the 1998 film *Shakespeare in Love* (shown
above) suggests that people's fascination for
Shakespeare and his plays is very much alive.

🔲 THEATRE OF IDEAS

The German playwright Bertolt Brecht (1898–
1956) believed that plays should change the way
people think. He thought that audiences would
understand the message better if they were
constantly reminded that they were watching a
play, not reality. Among his best-known plays is
The Caucasian Chalk Circle (shown here), which
questions motherly love in a dispute over a child.

OSCAR WILDE

*The brilliantly witty Irish writer Oscar
Wilde (1854–1900) shot to fame and
fortune with his comic plays, notably* The
Importance of Being Earnest, *which
commented on the social 'manners' of the
time. Wilde was famous for his showy,
artistic behaviour and
looks – he wore a
green carnation in
his buttonhole on
the opening night of
his plays. But after
three famous trials, he
died in exile in Paris.*

Non-fiction

NOVELS and short stories are described as 'fiction' – they portray imaginary worlds. The opposite is 'non-fiction' – books about real things, activities, people or events. Books on history, science, geography, religion, gardening, cooking, nature, art and sport, are all non-fiction. Reference books such as these, and encyclopedias and dictionaries, must be precise, accurate and easy to understand. History, biographies of famous people and travel books have to be factually correct, yet also well written to hold their readers' attention.

◢ DICTIONARIES

The earliest dictionaries simply listed foreign words and their meanings. But in 1755, Dr Samuel Johnson (1709–84) defined the words of his own language, in his *Dictionary of the English Language*.

◢ KEEPING A RECORD

By keeping diaries and letters, writers have provided the world with important information and opinions about events that happened in their lifetime. Samuel Pepys (1633–1703), an English government official in London, kept a diary from 1660 to 1669. As well as details of his personal life, it records eyewitness accounts of major events, such as the Great Fire of London of 1666, shown in this painting.

HISTORY

The ancient Greeks developed the art of history writing and passed it on to the Romans. Julius Caesar (c.100–44 BC) was not just a brilliant Roman general and leader, but a great war historian.

◢ TRAVEL WRITING

Some of the most fascinating non-fiction recounts explorers' adventures through strange lands. The great Norwegian polar explorer Roald Amundsen (1878–1928) described his famous journey in 1911 in his book *The South Pole*.

Giant Tortoise

GENOVESA

MARCHENA

Green Sea turtle

SAN SALVADOR

GALAPAGOS FINCHES

RABIDA

BALTRA

FERNANDINA

PINZON

PACIFIC OCEAN

Galapagos Penguin

SANTA CRUZ

SANTA FE   Giant Tortoise

ISABELA

The Beagle

SAN CRISTOBAL

THE GALAPAGOS ISLANDS

Fur Seal

SANTA-MARIA

ESPANOLA

0 10 20 30
km

☐ BIG NEW IDEAS

When the young British scientist Charles Darwin (1809–82) visited the Galapagos Islands, off South America, in 1835, he noticed how the animals had adapted physically to suit the conditions on each island. This helped him to formulate his theory of evolution, published in *The Origin of Species* (1859), a book that changed the way we look at the history of life on Earth.

water vapour condenses, forming water droplets

plants give off water

☐ BOOKS FOR LEARNING

Making information interesting and fun to learn is a major challenge. The information has to be clear and well presented. Illustrations drawn to go with the text, such as this diagram of the water cycle, can help explain a difficult subject. A 'glossary' explains terms and an index allows readers to find a subject quickly.

water from oceans and lakes evaporates

☐ ANNE FRANK'S DIARY

Anne Frank (1929–45) was a German Jewish girl who, during Word War II, spent two years hiding with her family from the Nazis in a secret apartment in Amsterdam. In 1944 they were betrayed, and Anne died in Belsen concentration camp. Her diary is one of the most vivid documents about the suffering inflicted by the Nazi regime.

Children's books

SOME of the most famous works of literature written during the 19th and 20th centuries were written for children. Authors who successfully capture a child's imagination can lead the reader into extraordinary imaginary worlds – children's books are often more inventive than adult fiction. Pictures, or illustrations, can also help to fire the imagination and can play a large part in the success of children's books. Pictures in the original *Alice in Wonderland* were by the illustrator John Tenniel (1820–1914).

◨ STORIES WITH MORALS

Fables are stories that feature animals who behave like humans, and give a clear moral lesson. In *The Hare and the Tortoise*, a fable by Aesop (an ancient Greek writer who lived about 620 to 560 BC), the speedy, boastful hare is so confident of winning a race against the tortoise that he goes to sleep. The slow-but-steady tortoise wins the race!

◨ FAIRY TALES

The son of a poor shoemaker, storyteller Hans Christian Andersen (1805–75) became Denmark's most famous author, known above all for his fairy tales. He wrote more than 150 in all, including *The Ugly Duckling*, *The Snow Queen*, and *The Wild Swans* (shown here).

◨ ALICE IN WONDERLAND

To amuse 10-year-old Alice Liddell and her sisters, Lewis Carroll (1832–98) – a mathematics teacher at Oxford University – invented a series of strange and fanciful stories, published as *Alice's Adventures in Wonderland* and *Through the Looking Glass*. Here, Alice is having tea with the Mad Hatter and his friends.

TREASURE ISLAND

One of the most memorable characters in children's fiction is Long John Silver, the one-legged pirate in Treasure Island, *by British author Robert Louis Stevenson (1850–94). He nearly succeeds in cheating the boy hero Jim Hawkins in the quest to recover the buried treasure.*

◪ THE WIZARD OF OZ

The Wonderful Wizard of Oz, written in 1899 by American Frank L. Baum (1856–1919), is a fairy tale about finding your heart's desire: courage, brains, a heart and home. It was made into a hugely successful film in 1939.

◪ COLLECTORS OF FAIRY TALES

Many of the most famous fairy tales were folk stories that have been collected and retold. The French poet Charles Perrault (1628–1703) made popular such favourites as *Cinderella* (shown here) and *Sleeping Beauty*. Other favourites, including *Hansel and Gretel*, were collected by the German brothers Jakob (1785–1863) and Wilhelm Grimm (1786–1859).

◪ WILLIE WONKA

Charlie and the Chocolate Factory is one of the funny and imaginative books by British author Roald Dahl (1916–90). The film version was renamed *Willie Wonka and the Chocolate Factory*.

Science fiction

DURING the 19th century, people started to speculate as to how science and new technology might change the world. Authors such as Jules Verne and H.G. Wells wrote stories about future worlds equipped with new machines. This kind of writing has now developed into the specialized field of writing called science fiction. And, just as science and technology have become infinitely more complex and sophisticated since the 19th century, so too has science fiction.

H.G.WELLS' WAR OF THE WORLDS

Color by **Technicolor**

A MIGHTY PANORAMA OF EARTH-SHAKING FURY!

TWO YEARS IN THE MAKING!

NOTHING SO SPECTACULAR EVER PUT ON FILM BEFORE!

PRODUCED BY GEORGE PAL WHO GAVE YOU 'DESTINATION MOON' & 'WHEN WORLDS COLLIDE'

THE WAR OF THE WORLDS

◪ FATHER OF SCIENCE FICTION

The first writer to bring futuristic science to novels was the French author Jules Verne (1828–1905). His books centred on travel adventures, notably *Journey to the Centre of the Earth* (this scene is from the 1959 film version) and *Twenty Thousand Leagues under the Sea.*

◪ *BRAVE NEW WORLD*

A nightmarish vision of the future was created by British novelist Aldous Huxley (1894–1963) in *Brave New World* (this scene is from the US TV series). In a 25th-century world, humans are hatched in incubators and lead trouble-free lives, at the cost of all individual freedom.

◪ H.G. WELLS

British author Herbert George Wells (1866–1946) believed that advances in science might create a better world. He wrote a series of highly successful science-fiction novels, such as *The First Men in the Moon* and *The Time Machine*. In *The War of the Worlds* (made into a film in 1953), he envisaged Martians invading Earth and landing in the United States.

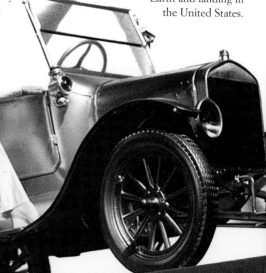

2001: A SPACE ODYSSEY

The British science-fiction author Arthur C. Clarke (b. 1917) made some remarkable predictions, including satellite communication. The 1968 film *2001: A Space Odyssey* (pictured below), based on his screenplay and short story, includes many predictions, such as interplanetary space travel and a talking, intelligent computer.

ISAAC ASIMOV

A key figure in the development of science fiction was the Russian-born American writer and biochemist, Isaac Asimov (1920–92). He is best known for his Foundation *trilogy, written in the early 1950s, which traces the collapse and revival of a futuristic interstellar empire. Asimov wrote some 500 books in total, including many books on science.*

THE FIRST ROBOTS

The word 'robot' (from the Czech word for forced labour) was invented in 1920 by the Czech novelist and playwright Karel Čapek (1890–1938). In his play *R.U.R. (Rossum's Universal Robots)*, a scientist invents human-like machines that come to dominate the world and threaten to wipe out the human race. Today people can make their own robots, like this 'Mindstorms' toy.

BIG BROTHER

The novel *Nineteen Eighty-Four*, written in 1948 by British author George Orwell (1903–50), and made into a film in 1984, gave the world a frightening vision of the future (now our past!). It describes a Britain where all independent thought is monitored and controlled by the government: 'Big Brother is watching you'.

The power of the word

SOME books carry such a powerful message that they have the power to change the course of history. The ideas of the German philosopher Karl Marx (1818–83), published in *The Communist Manifesto* and *Das Kapital*, for example, resulted in several revolutions and transformed the lives of millions of people around the world. On a smaller scale, Arthur Conan Doyle's descriptions of analyzing crime scenes – in his novels about the fictional detective Sherlock Holmes – had an important influence on police methods and detective work at the beginning of the 20th century.

◤ THE TRUTH ABOUT WORLD WAR I

During World War I, soldiers lived in wretched conditions in the trenches that faced each other along the Western Front in France and Belgium. Thousands died in single battles. Their families knew little of this horror until it was described in 1929 in *All Quiet on the Western Front*, a novel by the German writer Erich Maria Remarque (1898–1970).

◣ UNCLE TOM'S CABIN

Slavery was part of life in the Southern states until the American Civil War of 1861–65. The cruelty of slavery had been exposed in the novel *Uncle Tom's Cabin* by the writer Harriet Beecher Stowe (1811–96). Published in 1852, the book played a major part in encouraging opposition to slavery.

◤ GULLIVER'S TRAVELS

The fantasy-adventure story about Gulliver in the lands of miniature people and giants, by the British author Jonathan Swift (1667–1745), is a witty satire on human foolishness. It mocks the words and deeds of politicians, scientists and philosophers.

CRY, THE BELOVED COUNTRY

In 1948, the first novel by the South African writer Alan Paton (1903–88) brought to world attention the cruelty and injustices of 'apartheid'. This official government policy separated people of different races in South Africa, and limited the rights of the majority black population. A film version was made in 1995.

THE GRAPES OF WRATH

During the 1930s, a drought in the American Midwest turned much of the farmland into a 'Dust Bowl'. Ruined farmers fled to California, where they took up work as fruit pickers. *The Grapes of Wrath,* by the American writer John Steinbeck (1902–68), aroused much public sympathy for their hardship and misery. The book was made into a film in 1940.

BLACK BEAUTY

This popular children's book by the British author Anna Sewell (1820–78) is about a beautiful black horse that suffers in cruel hands before eventually finding a happy home. It helped in improving the way people in Britain treated their horses.

MAO'S 'LITTLE RED BOOK'

During the 1960s, some 800 million copies of the *Quotations from Chairman Mao* were distributed to everyone in China. These words of wisdom from Mao-Zedong (1893–1976), the Chinese Communist leader, inspired fanatical support for Mao during his 'Cultural Revolution'. However, the revolution turned out to be a political disaster.

L
I
T
E
R
A
T
U
R
E

Publishing

BOOKS remain a key source of information and entertainment in our world. Hundreds of thousands of new books are published every year. Almost all of them are produced by publishing companies. Publishers select the best books from among the many that authors send to them, or they commission authors to write books for them. The Internet will bring big changes to the world of books; new kinds of literature may develop, perhaps combining music and film. But these too will have to entertain their audience successfully and hold its attention, just as the old storytellers did when literature first began.

◩ BESTSELLERS

The bestselling book of all time is the Bible. Over the centuries, about six billion copies of the Bible have been sold. The aim of most publishers is to create bestsellers!

◪ AUTHORS

Authors are the starting point for most books. Before they start writing, they may spend many weeks researching their subject and making notes on how to shape the content of the book. Some write out their work by hand, others use a computer, and they often make many revisions along the way. Most authors agree that writing is: '10 percent inspiration and 90 percent hard work'.

◪ EDITORS AND DESIGNERS

At the publisher's office, an editor goes through the author's text, correcting any errors, making suggestions for changes, and questioning anything that is not clear. A designer plans how the pages will look. He or she chooses the size and style for the type, and for illustrated books works out where to position the pictures and text so that they are closely linked. The designer also briefs the illustrator on what the pictures need to show.

☑ ILLUSTRATORS

Book illustrators are artists who specialize in turning ideas into visual images. They generally work on books of a particular kind, for example children's storybooks, reference books like this one, or complex scientific publications. Following the designer's instructions, the illustrator usually produces pencil sketches (called 'roughs') first, for approval, before painting the final illustrations.

E-BOOKS

Novels and other electronic books (e-books) can be downloaded from the Internet to your home computer. Soon it may be possible to read them on portable, booklike screens. We may be on the threshold of an entirely new age of literature.

⊐ PRINTING

Before a book is printed, the pages are sent in electronic form to a 'reproduction house', where they are made into films. Some printers now print from electronic files instead of films. This method of printing is called CTP (Computer to Plate). The printer prepares metal plates which are attached to rollers. These are inked, and large sheets of paper are run through the machine (shown here). The sheets are then folded, trimmed and bound.

☑ BOOKSHOPS AND LIBRARIES

Printed books are stored in a publisher's warehouse. Booksellers and libraries order the books they want to stock from the publisher. Bookshops choose books that they think will appeal to their bookbuyers. Libraries hold a greater range of information and learning, and are an key element of the civilized world.

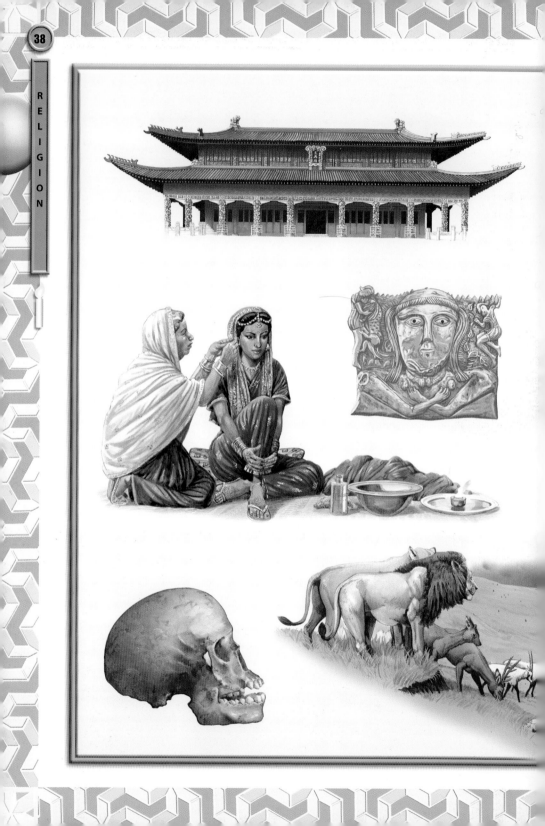

Religion

RELIGION is a way of making sense of the world. It can give people meaning and purpose to their lives, and provide hope of continued existence after death. Many religions make laws encouraging good behaviour, but religious disagreements have also led to wars. No one is sure when religious beliefs began, but many archaeologists suggest they may have originated with the first languages about two million years ago. Once early humans had learned to communicate practical needs, it was probably not long before they were able to express deeper feelings and religious ideas.

Seeking God

RELIGIOUS experiences are some of the most powerful known to humankind. They can range from visions of divine beings to a sense of inner peace. Over the centuries, they have inspired believers to perform acts of heroism and compassion – but they have also sparked bitter wars. People seek to make contact with their God, or gods, in different ways. Some go on pilgrimage to holy places; some meditate on the wonders of the world. Others use the teachings of their faith in their lives. In this way, the smallest action becomes a religious experience, and a way of showing devotion to God.

◪ OUT OF THIS WORLD

The world can be a magical, mysterious place, and human feelings can be so powerful that it seems impossible for them to disappear completely at death. Many religions teach that after death our souls live on outside the body, finding eternal peace with God.

LIVING BY FAITH

In the past, most people had religious faith. They relied on religion to explain life's mysteries. Today, many people choose to rely on scientific knowledge. But many people still believe in the soul, or spirit, which science still cannot fully explain.

◪ HOLY PLACES

Almost all religions have special holy places, where priests hold rituals and make offerings and where worshippers can pray and ask for help from their gods. This Chinese temple is decorated with prayers written in red and gold. In China, these are the traditional colours of good luck and blessings.

☑ A MESSAGE FROM GOD?

Since ancient times, people all around the world have interpreted dramatic natural events such as storms and sunsets as messages from the gods. Some religions honour nature gods, who control the Sun, Moon, winds, waves and weather. Others worship one great creator-God, maker and sustainer of the whole Universe.

☑ AWE AND WONDER

The beauty of the natural world, including delicate creatures like this butterfly, have inspired countless people with feelings of awe and wonder. Religious teachers from many faiths encourage their followers to respect the natural environment. They ask us to honour and respect all living things, because they believe them to be made by God.

☑ SYMBOLS OF FAITH

Sacred symbols are used to identify members of different faiths. A six-pointed star was used as a seal by Jewish King David (ruled c.1010–970 BC). Today, a blue Star of David forms part of the Israeli national flag.

☑ A GRAND DESIGN?

For thousands of years, religious people have asked questions such as 'why was I born?' and 'what is the meaning of life?' Seeing plants and animals living in carefully balanced ecosystems makes us wonder whether we also form part of a grand design. Is human existence planned and guided by God, or are we free to think and act as we choose?

Mystery and magic

THE details of early religions have not survived. But we can still detect traces of them today among peoples who live like the first humans, as hunters and gatherers – for example, in the Amazon rainforests of South America. For early humans, it seems that the world was full of mystery and magic. It was a holy place, in which gods, humans, and the whole natural environment were closely linked together and were dependent on one another. Everything – men, women, plants, rocks, animals, and even the weather – had a spirit or soul that must be honoured. Many early peoples also believed in a supreme god, and in other supernatural beings.

◁ BURIED WITH CARE

This human skull was buried in the Grimaldi Caves in Italy about 28,000 years ago. It was decorated with red ochre, a paint made from red earth. The decoration was probably a sign of honour or respect, and may indicate that the people who buried the skull believed in life after death.

▱ SHARING SPIRIT POWER

Magnificent cave paintings like this one of a bison were painted on the walls of a cave at Lascaux in southern France about 17,000 years ago, and hundreds of similar paintings were found in caves nearby. The pictures were probably created to honour the spirits of wild animals. Early people may have used them in religious rituals.

▱ PROTECTIVE MAGIC

The Celtic civilization flourished in many parts of Europe from about 800 BC to AD 100. This Celtic warrior's skin and shield are painted with magic and sacred designs. The Celts believed that religion and magic could help protect them in battle.

LIFE AFTER DEATH

People from many civilizations – from South America to Siberia – have aimed to help people's spirits survive by carefully preserving their dead bodies. But the best-known examples of this religious custom are probably Egyptian mummies (left).

▢ PAST AND PRESENT

This 19th-century painting of Australian Aboriginals records a ceremony called a corroboree that originated many thousands of years ago. By singing and dancing, the people called on sacred spirits to help their community and make it strong. Aboriginals still preserve many ancient traditions, including religious rituals.

▢ IN HARMONY WITH NATURE

Traditionally, native peoples of North and South America believed that the natural and supernatural worlds were closely linked. They honoured many 'holy' places, where they believed they could make contact with gods and spirits, and they prayed to natural forces such as the wind and rain to help them survive.

▣ MYSTERIOUS MONUMENT

The stone passage grave at Newgrange in Ireland was built about 3100 BC. The tomb builders deliberately positioned the round doorway so that it would channel the Sun's rays into the burial chamber just once a year, at midwinter. This may have had some religious meaning, but no written evidence has survived to tell us what it might be.

Ancestor spirits

TRADITIONAL religions taught that spirits of dead ancestors continued to play an important part in the world. They possessed (took over) family members, who fell into a trance and spoke with the spirit's voice. They offered advice or warnings, and made demands. Believers thought that the spirits within them had the power to heal or harm. They tried to please ancestor spirits by building shrines where they could 'feed' them with food, water or blood. They summoned them through rituals and dances, then, when the spirits' work was done, performed exorcisms (special ceremonies) to drive them away.

◨ ROYAL REVERENCE

In the ancient kingdom of Benin in West Africa, beautiful brass and bronze altar statues were made to commemorate dead kings. People believed that the spirits of dead kings could survive in the hearts and minds of rulers that were still alive.

◪ ANCESTOR STORY

This dancer from the Aranda Aboriginal people of central Australia is retelling an ancient myth. It describes how his ancestors fought against two man-eating eagles that attacked his tribe. He is wearing strings of eagle feathers, and a feathered head-dress. The bunches of leaves he is holding represent an eagle's wings.

◀ THE POWER OF THE DEAD

Traditionally, the Hemba people of Zaire carved wooden statues, called *singiti*, of their dead ancestors. They believed that by offering the statues food and prayers, they could connect with their ancestors' spirits, and that this would give them power to heal illness or help hunters find food.

HALLOWEEN

In Christian Europe and North America, children celebrate Halloween (the night before All Saints' Day) by dressing up as witches and making ghostly pumpkin lanterns. In the past, people believed that the spirits of the dead left their graves at Halloween to wander.

◨ MEN OR MONSTERS?

Square, bronze containers made in ancient China more than 3000 years ago held food and drink offered as sacrifices to ancestor spirits. The vessels were decorated with faces of *taotie* – fierce monsters with claws and horns. Historians think that *taotie* originated as pictures of male ancestors, but that over the years the human faces began to be portrayed as monsters – probably, because early people feared that ancestor spirits might haunt them or do them harm.

◨ ANCESTOR GIFTS

The traditional faith of Japan is called Shinto (the Way of the Gods). Followers worship nature spirits and also the spirits of dead ancestors, which they believe can protect them. Shinto priests hold rituals to please ancestor spirits and light lanterns and make offerings at holy shrines. Today, favourite gifts include flowers and *sake* (rice wine).

◨ TALL TOTEM

'Totems' are spirit helpers. They can be special animals with magic powers, or the spirits of dead ancestors, shamans and heroes. Native Americans from northwestern North America shape the trunks of tall trees into towering totem poles that stand outside the homes of high-ranking families. Each pole tells the history of a particular family, commemorating brave deeds by dead ancestors, or stories and legends about family members. They may also portray the family's special totem animal, such as this huge eagle.

Shamans and sacrifices

OVER the centuries, one of the most important religious questions people have asked is 'how can we make contact with our gods'? In northeast Asia and the Americas, magicians and healers known as shamans were able to enter a strange state of mind – by chanting, fasting or sometimes taking powerful herbs – in which they felt like they were flying through the air or diving deep underground. They believed these disturbing experiences allowed them to leave their bodies and enter the land of the spirits. There, traditionally, the shamans learned valuable new knowledge, fought with evil forces and spoke to the gods. People also tried to make contact with their gods by offering them gifts or sacrifices. They hoped the gods would send them blessings in return.

◤ SEEKING SPIRITS

Shamans asked sacred spirits to make sure the seasons arrived on time, and that there was enough food for families to survive. This shaman from Mongolia is carrying a drum, for summoning spirits and lulling humans into a trance.

◀ SELF – SACRIFICE

Viking legends told how Odin, the shaman god of wisdom, sought knowledge by sacrificing himself to himself. For nine days and nights, he hung in agony from the branches of an ash tree, until he had learned magic secrets. Like other shamans, he had spirit-helpers – two ravens, called Thought and Memory, who flew beside him wherever he went.

◪ IN DISGUISE

Sometimes shamans disguise themselves to help them pass more easily into the spirit world. At other times, they put on disguises to embody powerful nature spirits, or to act out the events they want to make happen. This shaman from the Asmat region of Africa is wearing an elaborate spirit mask that covers him from head to foot.

LIFE AND POWER

The Aztecs, who were powerful in Central America from AD 1300–1521, believed that they had to 'feed' their gods, or else the world would end. They sacrificed captives at pyramid-temples, letting their blood flow down the steps.

◩ SHARING ANIMAL POWER

This North American shaman, painted during the 19th century, is wearing furs and feathers taken from powerful wild animals such as bears and eagles. Shamans believed they could draw strength from such animals – their spirit ancestors – and that this would help protect them in the dangerous spirit world.

◩ LIVING SPIRIT

Followers of many traditional beliefs often make models to represent the spirits they honour, or to act as homes for the spirits if they visit Earth. This Kachina, or spirit-figure, was made by the Hopi people of North America. The Hopi honour the spirits of the Sun, winds, rain and maize plants (their traditional staple food).

◩ HEALING POWERS

In many communities, shamans serve as counsellors and healers. People who are unwell consult them because they believe their illness is caused by evil spirits, and that the shaman has power to drive them away. Shamans, like this traditional healer from Africa, may use songs and rattles to frighten the spirits, or other 'magical' curing aids, such as bones and stones.

Nature gods

ABOUT 8000 BC, for the first time, people began to live as farmers in settled villages, rather than roaming the land as hunter gatherers. They grew plants and kept animals for food. This changed lifestyle led to the development of new religious beliefs. People began to think of Earth as their kindly, generous mother, and to honour the Sun, wind, and weather – together with important food plants – as gods and goddesses who controlled the natural world. If the crops withered or the rains failed, communities were struck by famine and many people died. So, at important seasons of the farming year, they made offerings and sacrifices to please all the different nature gods.

◪ SPIRIT OF THE RAIN

In ancient Japan, froglike nature spirits called Kami were believed to control the rain, winds and storms. According to Shinto – the traditional religion of Japan – Kami control all natural forces. They can be kind and gentle or fierce and very dangerous.

☑ HIDDEN AMONG TREES

Once families had settled in villages, woodland became a place of fear. In England, villagers dreaded meeting the Green Man – a sinister nature god who lived in the trees.

◪ POWER OVER NATURE

Many peoples used religious rituals and magic ceremonies to try to win influence over the natural world. Native Americans performed ritual dances, with the aim of attracting buffalo to the hunting grounds close to their villages or tipi camps. Young men in buffalo costumes danced day and night, until lookouts announced that buffalo had been sighted. The buffalo were then killed for food and their skins.

◻ GUNDESTROP BOWL

Celtic civilization flourished throughout Europe from about 800 BC to AD 100. The Celts worshipped many nature gods, and also blended their own religious ideas with earlier traditions and with the beliefs of peoples living nearby.

This goddess was pictured on a famous piece of Celtic metalwork, the Gundestrop bowl, which was made in eastern Europe.

SHINING SUN GOD

The Inca people, who lived in the Andes mountains of Peru (AD 1100s–1532), worshipped Inti, the golden god of the Sun. He brought light and warmth every day, protecting the Inca and helping their crops to grow.

◻ LORD OF THE LIFE-GIVING RAIN

Food crops, such as wheat in the Middle East and maize in Central America, were so important for early farmers that they became like gods. The life-giving rain that helped them grow was also worshipped. This clay statue, made between AD 600–900, portrays a rain god honoured by the Maya people, who lived in the rainforests of Central America.

◻ GOD OF THUNDER

Early farmers dreaded thunderstorms, which could flatten their crops and wipe out the harvest. Many worshipped gods who they believed controlled thunder, like Thor, the mighty Viking god of storms. Legend tells how Thor rode through the clouds in his chariot, brandishing a great thunderbolt.

Gods, heroes and kings

BY ABOUT 3500 BC, some villages had grown into the first cities, ruled by powerful kings. City dwellers practiced many new skills – there were weavers and potters, metal workers, soldiers, merchants and tax collectors. New forms of religion developed to meet the people's needs. They worshipped their city's unique guardian god, or the gods and goddesses who protected their special craft. In ancient Egypt and the Middle East, the people believed that kings, queens and local heroes were divine. All these gods were worshipped in new kinds of buildings – huge temples, designed as holy homes for them, where they were served by priests.

LION-KILLER

The ancient Greek hero Heracles (son of Zeus, king of the gods) was said to be 'superhuman'. He performed twelve dangerous 'labours', or tasks, one of which was killing the Nemean Lion – a man-eating monster. After completing his labours, the gods rewarded him with immortality.

GOD, PRIEST OR KING?

This statue of a dignified bearded man was found in the ruined city of Mohenjo-Daro, in the Indus Valley (in the far northwest of the Indian subcontinent). It was made about 2200 BC by the rich and technologically advanced civilization that flourished there. The statue is thought to portray either a god, a priest or a king – or perhaps a powerful man who was honoured as all of these. We cannot tell for certain, because no one has yet been able to decipher the mysterious system of writing used by scribes of the Indus Valley culture.

HERO-KING

Gilgamesh, king of the city of Etrech, features in many myths and legends from the ancient Middle East. Some are more than 4000 years old. He was said to be two thirds god, one third man.

☑ HOLY KNOWLEDGE

Writing, which developed in many parts of the world after about 3000 BC, enabled religious ideas and stories to be recorded permanently. For many centuries only a few well-educated people (usually priests) knew how to read and write. This is a scribe from the Mayan civilization of Central America.

☑ SEAT OF POWER

This wood-carving shows a Yoruba king from West Africa. Traditionally, the Yoruba people worshipped many different gods, including Olorun (Lord of the Sky), orishas (life-giving forces), ancestors, and nature spirits. Many Yoruba kings claimed kinship with the orishas.

◪ EGYPTIAN OFFERINGS

The ancient Egyptians believed that their kings, whom they called pharaohs, were the children of gods – especially the Sun god Amun-Ra and the cow-headed mother-goddess Hathor. Half-human, half-divine, the pharaohs formed a living link between the gods and ordinary people.

◪ CHOSEN BY GOD

Many groups of people, as well as individuals, have believed that they were specially chosen by God. He was their special protector and saviour. If they worshipped Him and obeyed His laws, He would take care of them. The Bible tells the story of Noah, who obeyed God's command to build an ark, or large ship, in which to house his family and one pair of all the animals in the world. God then sent a great flood to punish the world. Only Noah, his family, and the animals survived.

Hindus and Sikhs

HINDUISM is the religion of India. It originated about 1500 BC among the Aryan people of the northwest. About 1000 BC, the first Hindu holy books, the *Vedas*, were written down. These describe the gods and goddesses and record hymns and prayers. Since then, Hinduism has divided into many sects, but its essential beliefs remain the same. Hindus aim to escape from this world and unite their souls with Brahman by following *dharma* (the right way to live). Until they lead pure lives, Hindus believe they will be reborn in different bodies again and again. The Sikh faith was founded in 1499 by a Hindu named Guru Nanak. He believed that people were all children of the same god, and preached religious tolerance.

◀ **TEMPLES**
Many Hindus go to a *mandir*, or temple, to say prayers and make offerings of sweets and flowers. The temples are often beautifully decorated with carvings of gods and spirits. The name for a holy statue that represents a favourite goddess or god is a *murti*.

◣ **SIKH HOLY SHRINE**
The Golden Temple, or *Harimandar*, at Amritsar in India is built on the ground where Guru Nanak spent time meditating about God. It is a specially holy place for Sikhs.

◣ **THE RIVER OF HEAVEN**
To Hindus, the River Ganges, which flows through the city of Varanasi, is specially sacred. They call it the 'River of Heaven'. Hindus make pilgrimages to its banks to pray and worship. They also cremate, or burn, the bodies of the dead there, so that the dead person's soul – free from its body – can continue on its spiritual journey.

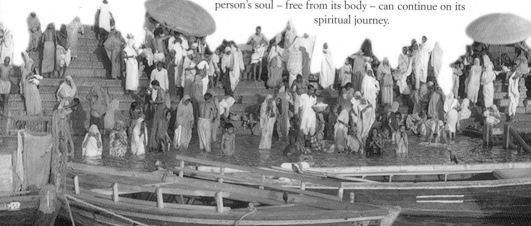

LIFE CYCLES

Like people from many different religions, Hindu familes mark important stages in each individual's life, such as weddings (below) and funerals, with prayers and religious ceremonies. They also believe that ordinary, everyday actions have a religious meaning. Each good deed takes a person closer to their spiritual goal, which is freedom from life in this world and union with Brahman, the supreme God.

SIKH SIGNS

Sikhs wear five special things to show their faith:
Kes = uncut hair
Kirpan = a small sword
Kara = a steel bangle
Kanga = a wooden comb
Kacch = white shorts

HINDU PRIEST

Hindu priests come from the highest caste, or rank, within Hindu society – they are Brahmins. There are also many Hindu spiritual teachers, or gurus. Priests and gurus teach important Hindu beliefs, including *dharma* (the right way to live), reincarnation (the soul's rebirth in a new body after death), and *karma* (the law of spiritual punishment and reward).

CELEBRATING THE SEASONS

Like people from many other faiths, Hindus hold festivals to celebrate the changing seasons. Holi is a Spring festival held in February or March. On the first day, people light bonfires. On the second day, they honour the playful god Krishna by playing practical jokes, such as throwing coloured powders or coloured water.

The way of Buddha

BUDDHA, or the Enlightened One, was the name given to Siddhartha Gautama, an Indian prince who lived from about 560 to 480 BC. As a young man he set out to travel the world, and was horrified to see so much suffering. Seeking to find a reason for it, he spent years meditating under a holy tree. People came to listen to his spiritual teaching and to ask his advice. The Buddha taught Four Noble Truths: 1) suffering is always part of life; 2) it is caused by greed or desire; 3) suffering (and life itself) will end when believers achieve *Nirvana* (perfect peace); and 4) *Nirvana* can be found by following the Eightfold Path of Buddhist study, prayer, and meditation. After the Buddha's death, his followers travelled throughout Southeast Asia spreading the news of his teachings in many lands.

◪ BUDDHIST MONK
Many Buddhist men and women decide to spend some time as monks or nuns, to learn more about their faith. This *bhikkhu*, or Buddhist monk, is studying holy scriptures.

◪ BOROBODUR
About AD 800, this huge centre of Buddhist worship was built at Borobodur on the island of Java, in Indonesia. It is the largest Buddhist holy building in the world. Six square terraces surround a central shrine. The walls of the lower terraces are covered with beautiful carvings portraying different aspects of the spiritual world.

◪ PALACE AND FORTRESS
Originally built as a fortress during the Middle Ages, the massive Potala Palace became the home of the Dalai Lamas, leaders of Buddhists in Tibet, during the 17th century. In 1959, the present Dalai Lama left the palace to live in India after Chinese troops took control of Tibetan lands.

A GUIDE FOR LIFE

Buddhists do not worship the Buddha as a god, but rather honour him as a guide who shows them the best way to live. There are many huge, splendid statues of the Buddha, carved from stone or cast from bronze or even pure gold. Buddhists leave offerings of flowers, incense and candles beside the statues.

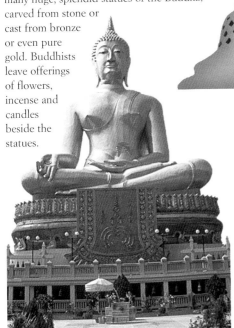

STUPAS

A stupa is a Buddhist monument. The first stupas were built to house the remains of the Buddha's body after he died. Later stupas were built to contain Buddhist holy writings or the bones of respected teachers and monks.

GARDENS FOR MEDITATION

Zen is a type of Buddhism popular in Japan. Its followers believe that meditation is the best way to reach spiritual peace and understanding. A Zen garden is made of raked sand, gravel and stones, where followers can sit quietly and focus their minds on meditation.

PAGODA IN BURMA

The spread of Buddhist teachings was encouraged by many kings and princes, who supported Buddhist monks and scholars and paid for magnificent Buddhist monuments. This beautiful temple in Burma is one of over 5000 Buddhist shrines built on the orders of King Anawrahta (ruled 1044–1077) and his descendants. Its tall pagoda towers have many separate layers, each one representing stages in a soul's progress toward *Nirvana*.

Confucius and Laozi

IN CHINA, the two most important religions are Confucianism and Daoism, both of which are based on moral teachings. Confucianism was founded by Kongfuzi, or Confucius (c.551–479 BC). Confucius was not concerned with worshipping gods, or with hopes of life after death. Instead, he taught people to live a good life, encouraging self control, hard work and respect for families. Daoism is based on the writings (called the *Daodejing*, or *The Way*) of philosopher Laozi, who lived about the same time as Confucius. Laozi described many gods, nature spirits and magical practices and encouraged meditation and spiritual harmony.

◪ **WATCHFUL GOD**
In China, many people who respect Confucian or Daoist teachings also believe in traditional gods, such as the 'Kitchen God'. He is believed to watch people as they go about their lives, and he reports wrong-doings to Heaven. His picture is kept in the kitchen.

◪ **WISE TEACHER**
Kongfuzi, or Confucius, encouraged his followers to be responsible, wise, and modest, and to show kindness and loyalty to others. Many of his wise sayings were written down by people who admired them. Today, millions of people in China and eastern Asia are still guided by his teachings.

◪ **RULERS' DUTIES**
Chinese emperors built many splendid temples, like this one in the 'Forbidden City' in Beijing. They visited the temples to make offerings on behalf of their people, asking the gods to send good harvests, peace, and prosperity. Confucius said that rulers should obey the 'will of heaven' by governing wisely and respecting the gods.

RESPECT

Traditionally, younger members of Chinese families show respect for elders, and women show respect for men – Confucius taught that the oldest man in a family was its head and should be obeyed. But mothers and grandmothers often have considerable power within a household, controlling almost everything that happens.

DAOISM

Laozi taught that there is a great power, known as Dao (the Way), that guides the Universe. His followers, called Daoists, try to live in harmony with Dao. This can mean living good lives, taking political action, or retreating to a wild place to be close to nature. Daoists use physical exercise and breathing techniques to bring their bodies closer to the life-force of Dao.

LIVING IN HARMONY

Daoists believe that the natural world is in a state of balance between two contrasting forces, Yin and Yang. Yin is cold, dark and female and Yang is hot, light and male. They are often represented by this black-and-white circular symbol. By following Dao (the Way), Daoists try to keep these forces in harmony.

A LASTING MEMORIAL

After Confucius died he was honoured almost like a god. A temple was built in the city of Qufu, Shandong Province, where he had lived. Prayers were said there, and offerings were made to his spirit. Over the years, Confucius's temple was enlarged and rebuilt by Chinese emperors as a sign of respect, until it became one of the most splendid religious buildings in all China.

Judaism

THE FOLLOWERS of three great religions – Judaism, Christianity and Islam – are often described as 'Peoples of the Book'. They all honour the same holy text, known as the Old Testament of the Bible, and respect the prophets, or religious teachers, whose actions are described in it. All three faiths originated in the Middle East, although today they have believers worldwide. Judaism is the oldest – it first developed about 2000 BC. Its followers believe in a single, all-powerful God, who created the world, freed the Jewish people from slavery in Egypt, led them to a Promised Land, known as Israel and set down laws (or commandments) telling them how to live good lives and set an example to others.

◪ CREATOR GOD

Jewish beliefs have inspired people from many faiths to produce dramatic and beautiful works of art. This painting shows God creating the first man and woman, Adam and Eve. According to Jewish tradition, the whole world and everything in it was created by God in six days. Adam was made from earth, and Eve was made from a rib bone in Adam's side.

◩ SIGNS OF FAITH

Some Jewish men wear special clothes as a sign of their faith. The *kippah* (or *yarmulke*) is a little cap that covers the crown of the head and is worn as a mark of respect for God. For praying, Jewish men may wear a *tallit*, or shawl.

A SCATTERED PEOPLE

For almost 2000 years, Jewish people were forced to live outside their traditional homeland in the Middle East. Some settled in Europe, but they were often persecuted. During the 19th century, many Jewish people emigrated to the United States, where they hoped to find religious freedom. Today, there is a Jewish state in Israel, and Jewish communities in many parts of the world.

PRAYING AT THE TEMPLE WALL

Jewish people stand to pray at the Western Wall in Jerusalem. This ancient structure is the only remaining part of the Temple in Jerusalem, a very holy place of worship founded by King Solomon almost 3000 years ago. Jewish people travel from all over the world to pray there.

SAVED BY A MIRACLE

Moses was a Jewish leader who lived about 1200 BC. God told him to lead the Jews out of Egypt. They were chased by Egyptian soldiers, but – according to Jewish scriptures – God parted the waters of the Red Sea so that Moses and the Jews could cross in safety. When the waters ran back, the Egyptians were drowned.

MEMORIAL FESTIVAL

Pesach, or Passover, is a Jewish festival held in March or April. It commemorates the time long ago when the Jews escaped from slavery in Egypt. At the beginning of the festival, Jewish families share a joyful meal and take part in a service called *seder*, with scripture readings and songs. Meals at *Pesach* include flatbread and herbs.

TEACHING

The Jewish scriptures are called the *Tenakh*. They are divided into three parts, the most important of which is the *Torah*, which means 'teaching'. This Jewish man is reading from the *Torah* in a synagogue. He has covered his head and shoulders to show respect.

Christianity

CHRISTIANITY originated in the Middle East in the first century AD. Jewish people there believed that a religious teacher named Jesus was 'the Messiah', a leader who would free them from Roman rule and bring them closer to God. Jesus respected the teachings of the Jewish prophets, but added his own message: the most important thing in life is to love God and to behave well towards other people. He was killed by the Romans as a danger to public order, but Christians believe he came back to life three days later. They also believe that people who follow his teachings will live after death.

◩ THE CHRISTMAS STORY

Christians believe that Jesus was born in a stable in Bethlehem, to Mary, a virgin, and her future husband Joseph, a carpenter. Three Wise Men, led by a star, travelled from the east to worship Jesus. They gave him gifts of gold, frankincense and myrrh.

LIGHT IN DARKNESS

At Christingle – a service that looks forward to Jesus's birth at the darkest time of the year – children carry a decorated orange. The orange represents the world, and the candle stands for the 'light' (joy and peace) that Jesus brought to the world.

◰ ALONE WITH GOD

From the beginnings of Christianity, some Christian men and women have chosen to retreat to remote places, such as this mountaintop in Greece, so that they can devote their lives to God. There, in monasteries or convents, they spend their lives in prayer and study.

◄ SPREADING THE GOOD NEWS

Over the centuries, missionaries have carried news of the Christian faith – the Gospel – to countries all over the world. The missionaries shown here are preaching to people in India, in about 1850. Many missionaries built schools and hospitals for the people whom they hoped to persuade to become Christians. Today, there are groups of Christians in almost every country.

◄ NEW CHRISTIANS

Crowds of Christian believers belonging to the Zion Church meet for worship in South Africa. In Europe, many people turned away from organized Christian churches during the 20th century. But in Africa many varieties of Christian worship are thriving. The Zion Church has over seven million members.

◄ FIT FOR A BISHOP

The Christian Church is led by bishops (senior priests). Each bishop has a home church, called a cathedral. These are often rich, splendid buildings. The cathedral in Moscow, capital city of Russia, is decorated with painted and gilded onion-shaped domes.

◄ A NEW LIFE

Many Christian churches hold a special ceremony, called baptism, to welcome new believers. The person being baptized is sprinkled with water (or sometimes bathed) to show that their old life has been washed away and their new Christian life has begun. Some churches only baptize adults; others baptize babies. Although a baby is too young to understand the ceremony, its parents and their close friends, chosen to be 'godparents' make a promise to bring the child up as a Christian.

Islam

THE FIRST Muslims (believers in Islam) lived in Arabia in the 7th century AD. They were followers of the Prophet Muhammad (c. AD 570–632), a religious teacher who received a series of revelations from God. These were written down to form a holy book, the *Qu'ran*, which is honoured as a guide and inspiration by Muslims today. The Prophet Muhammad worshipped a single God, the judge of all human behaviour. He also respected earlier Jewish prophets, including Jesus, as being messengers from God. Muslims believe that God will send no more prophets after Muhammad. They obey five rules: 1) belief in God and love for Muhammad; 2) prayer five times a day; 3) fasting during the month of Ramadan; 4) Hajj (pilgrimage to Mecca); and 5) *zakat* (giving to charity).

◩ ACROSS THE DESERT

Muslim traders, scholars and soldiers travelled long distances across the desert by camel. They carried the faith of Islam with them to many parts of Asia, North and West Africa, and the Middle East.

◩ CALL TO PRAYER

Mosques are buildings where Muslims meet to pray and to listen to readings from their holy book, the *Qu'ran*. They traditionally have at least one tall tower, called a minaret, next to the main building. From a platform at the top, a muezzin – an official with a loud, clear voice – calls Muslims to prayer. In many countries today the call to prayer is broadcast through loudspeakers.

◩ RELIGIOUS DUTIES

Islam teaches that it is a religious duty to pray five times a day. Muslim men bow down to the ground in prayer, kneeling on a prayer mat. They face in the direction of Mecca, the holy city of Islam.

HOLY CITY

For Muslims, Mecca (or Makkah) in Arabia is the most sacred city in the world. At its heart stands the Grand Mosque, containing the Ka'aba – an ancient cube-shaped holy structure draped in black and gold. All Muslims hope to make a pilgrimage to Mecca at least once in their lives.

RELIGIOUS DESIGNS

Muslim craftworkers excel in creating beautiful abstract designs, like the geometric patterns painted on the ceramic tiles that decorate this mosque. Similar designs decorate manuscripts, pottery and carpets. Islam teaches that it is wrong to make images of living things, since only Allah (God) can create life.

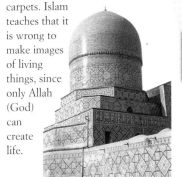

THE MUSLIM CALENDAR

Muslim history starts in AD 622, when Muhammad left Mecca to establish the first Muslim community in Medina. Muslims measure months and years by the Moon. Each month has 29 or 30 days.

DOME OF THE ROCK

The Dome of the Rock is a beautiful mosque in Jerusalem, a city (in present-day Israel) that is holy to Muslims, Christians and Jews. Inside is a large natural rock, from which, Muslims believe, Muhammad made a miraculous night journey to heaven to see Allah (God) on his throne.

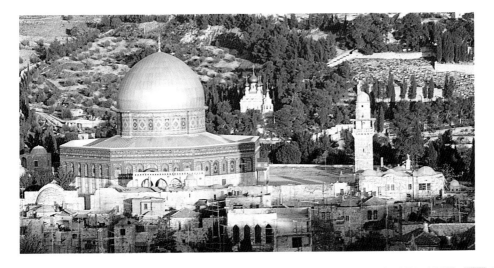

New Age

DURING the 20th century, traditional religions became less popular in many parts of the world. Many people stopped believing in God and chose not to go to churches, temples or other holy places to worship. However, most people did not completely lose their belief in a greater holy power. Some people revived mysterious religions from ancient times, re-creating their rituals. Some invented new religions of their own. Many of these were linked to nature worship, spiritual healing or faith in pseudo (fake) science. They searched for an alternative lifestyle that would unite mind, body and spirit, and looked forward to the dawning of a New Age, when men and women would bring peace and love to the Universe, and find the god within themselves.

☑ MIND, BODY AND SPIRIT

Followers of 'New Age' philosophies seek to balance mind, body, and spirit. Often they borrow techniques for exercise and meditation from ancient Asian religious traditions. This diagram shows some of the ideas of reiki, a Japanese religious teaching, whose believers aim to live in harmony with the Universal Life Force.

☑ HOLY HERITAGE

The huge stone circle at Stonehenge in southwest England has been a holy site for more than 3000 years. After centuries of neglect, it has once more become a place of worship. Druids (men and women who re-enact ancient Celtic ceremonies) and people seeking 'New Age' spiritual experiences travel there at midsummer to honour the Sun as it rises.

VOICES OF PROTEST

In 1980, in Poland, a group of organized workers (a trade union) called Solidarity was formed. It pressed for changes in the government, and within eight years, the group had 10 million members – too many for the government to overpower. The Polish government eventually had to accept many of Solidarity's demands, and in 1989, Solidarity received a large number of votes in the first free election. This union of people inspired people to strive for more freedom, almost like a religion.

CHURCH AND COMMERCE

In recent times, church leaders have joined a worldwide protest against the way that governments and big businesses control the world economy. They are demanding fair trade deals with people from developing countries, and the cancellation of international debts.

SAVING THE TREES

For many New Age sympathizers, protecting the natural environment from destruction has become a spiritual quest. They hold ceremonies to celebrate nature's beauty, and campaign to save fragile environments, such as rain forests, from harm.

GOOD CAUSES

Traditionally, all the world's faiths have encouraged charity. Increasingly, nonreligious people also help good causes. In 1984 and 1985, vast concerts raised over £100 million for famine relief in Africa.

A MODERN SAINT?

Diana, Princess of Wales (1961–97), became famous for the work she did to help people who were ill, injured or outcast. Some people called her a 'modern saint', but religious leaders did not approve of this title.

Replacing religion?

IN THE early years of a new millennium, many people are wondering what the future holds for the religions of the world. New scientific discoveries and secular (worldly) political ideas pose a powerful challenge to the power of old beliefs. New causes such as the Green Movement provide an alternative to religion for many people. New trends in society, such as individualism and materialism (love of things), mean that consumers look for pleasure and satisfaction here and now, rather than hoping to find peace and joy in a future life, after death. Faced with these challenges, will traditional faiths continue to exist or will they fade away?

◪ CONSUMER PASSIONS

Shopping has been described as the 'new religion' of people who seek happiness in material possessions. Many traditional religions encourage people to give up 'good things' in the hope of enjoying eternal life in heaven.

◪ PLAYING GOD?

Dolly the sheep was born in Scotland in 1997. Created by scientists using genetic engineering techniques, she was the first mammal to be cloned (copied) from adult cells. Some people fear that scientists are starting to copy God's role of creator.

◪ KNOWLEDGE, NOT FAITH

This amazing photograph, taken through an electron microscope, shows the surface of a tick's skin magnified thousands of times. (A tick is a small bug related to spiders and crabs.) Modern scientific instruments allow us to explore the natural world in great detail. For many people, greater knowledge and understanding of the natural world has replaced their faith in a mysterious, magical God.

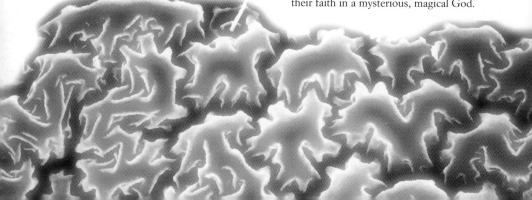

WHO MADE PEOPLE?

The 19th-century biologist Charles Darwin (1809–82) suggested that humans had developed from apes in a natural process called 'evolution'. At first thought a threat to religion, today his ideas are widely believed.

◪ FANATICAL FANS

In many parts of the world, sports fans follow their teams or the careers of sports superstars with the devotion that people in the past once gave to religion. Their loyalty is to a club and their fellow fans, not to beliefs or religious ideas.

◪ UNDERSTANDING THE UNIVERSE

In the late 1990s, supernovas (exploding stars) were photographed by the Hubble space telescope. For centuries, people thought of stars as signs of God's power. Modern space exploration has deepened some people's faith, but it has also increased respect for what human minds can achieve without the help of supernatural powers.

◪ INTOLERANCE?

Babies develop from a tiny collection of cells. Many religions teach that babies are gifts from God and should be loved. But in the future people may demand 'perfect' babies, designed by scientists.

Music

MUSIC is the most popular and widespread of all the arts. We whistle, hum and sing; we listen to music on the radio, on CD players. Many people learn to play musical instruments. Every nation and culture in the world has its own traditions of music. In the Western world, music developed into a highly complex art, involving orchestras of more than a hundred players. Fashions in music change all the time, and with them the instruments used to play it. These days, computers and electronic equipment can produce almost any kind of sound, and the most popular music in the world is often made by just a few musicians and singers. But the effect is similar: music appeals to our ears and emotions. It soothes or excites. It sets our imaginations alight.

Making music

MUSIC is the oldest of all the art forms. The very earliest humans discovered that certain objects – hollow tree trunks, different kinds of stone and the bones of large animals, for example – made curious ringing sounds when struck. A set of decorated mammoth bones found in a hut in Mezin, in the Ukraine, appears to have been used as musical instruments – a 20,000 year-old orchestra! Over time, the range of instruments increased. People jangled small bones as rattles; made drums from animal skins; and blew into hollow bamboo and bones to produce notes. Gradually these instruments were refined and standardized, and the skills needed to play them were taught to others.

◪ TAMBOURINE

A tambourine is a simple kind of drum made of animal skin stretched over a wooden frame. Metal disks inserted into gaps in the frame jangle when the tambourine is shaken. Tambourines were played in ancient Egypt, and were brought to Europe in medieval times during the Crusades.

◀ NAZCA DRUM

About 2000 years ago, the Nazca people of Peru in South America made elaborately painted pottery drums. It is thought that these were played during religious ceremonies. Such ceremonies may have been held on the site of the famous Nazca lines – vast patterns (many depicting animals) made from pathways marked out in the desert.

◪ STRINGED INSTRUMENTS

More than 4000 years ago, the ancient Egyptians played harps – called bow harps because of their shape – to accompany singers at funeral ceremonies. Pictures of them have been found on tomb walls. Harps and other instruments also formed small 'dance bands'.

THE FIRST INSTRUMENT

The oldest instrument of all is the human voice. From the beginning of human existence, human beings made calls to communicate (as do many other living creatures). As they developed their vocal cords for speech, no doubt they also began to explore the creative possibilities of sound by singing, perhaps accompanied by rhythmic clapping.

◪ DIDGERIDOO

The culture of the Australian Aborigines dates back some 50,000 years. The Aborigines most famous musical instrument is the didgeridoo. Traditional didgeridoos are made from tree trunks that have been hollowed out by termites. The deep droning sound is played to accompany singing and dancing.

◪ MAYAN WHISTLE

The Mayan civilization of Mexico and Central America, with its cities and soaring temple-pyramids, reached its peak between AD 600 and 900. This Mayan pottery whistle dates from this period. As with many early instruments, the maker has had fun by creating it in the form of a sculpture.

◪ PANPIPES

Ancient peoples discovered that tubes of different lengths produce different sounds when blown. Panpipes are made of a row of tubes bound together, each cut to a precise length to produce a specific note. The instrument is played by blowing across the tops of the tubes. Panpipes are named after the Greek god Pan, who is said to have made the first musical instrument from a reed.

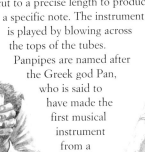

Percussion instruments

INSTRUMENTS that are struck are known as percussion instruments, from the Latin word *percutere*, meaning to hit'. After the human voice, they are the world's most ancient kind of instrument. The sound made by some percussion instruments – such as cymbals, xylophones and bells – comes from the ringing sound of the material from which they are made. Drums, on the other hand, have a sound box that amplifies, or increases, the sound made when the skin, or membrane, of the 'drumhead' is struck. Drums are used to beat out rhythms, but they can also be finely tuned to produce precise notes. The steel drums of Trinidad, for example, are made from empty oil drums and have carefully indented, dish-shaped tops that produce a scale of notes.

▲ AZTEC DRUM

During the 15th century, the Aztecs of Mexico made a drum called a *teponatzli* from a hollow log with a slot at the top. It was played with rubber-tipped drumsticks. Log drums give off a ringing sound that resonates around the empty space inside the log.

◼ SHINTO TEMPLE DRUM

Giant drums, accompanied by gongs and flutes, are used in the temple ceremonies of Japan's oldest religion, Shinto. The drums, called *wadaiko*, are still being made today. The largest one ever made was built in 1996. Made of wood and leather, its drumheads measure 1.8 metres across and it weighs 4 tons. In the past, temple drums also acted as warning sirens.

◻ AFRICAN DRUMS

Drums play a central role in African music, as this dancing troupe from Gambia indicates. A drummer can produce a complex pattern of rhythms and a wide range of sounds, from high, ringing notes near the edge to deeper booms nearer the middle.

◁ GAMELAN

Xylophones are percussion instruments, because the bars are struck with hammers. On the Indonesian island of Bali, the gamelan orchestras consist almost entirely of xylophones of various sizes. They play rippling music of great complexity, accompanying temple dancing and ceremonies. The music is not written down; it is learned by heart and takes years of practice.

▣ THE MODERN DRUM KIT

Bands, such this one accompanying Jon Bon Jovi in New York, use a drum kit that was developed in the 20th century. It generally consists of a large base drum operated by a foot pedal, tom toms, a larger floor tom and a snare drum (or side drum), which has springlike metal snares underneath that produce a rattling sound. The kit includes a set of cymbals. The 'hi-hat' cymbal is operated by another foot pedal.

CASTANETS

Flamenco dancers in Spain add tension and excitement to their movements by making rapid clicking sounds with castanets held in the palm of their hands. Castanets consist of a pair of wooden shells hinged together, rather like a clam.

▣ XYLOPHONE

African xylophones, like this one from Burkina Faso, are often made of wooden bars. Hard woods give off a bright, ringing tone. The sound is amplified by sound boxes, or resonators, underneath the bars. In traditional African xylophones, the resonators are often made from dried gourds – pumpkin-like vegetables.

Wind instruments

THE simplest kind of wind instrument is a plain tube. When the player blows into it, the air inside vibrates and produces a sound. The sound can be varied by altering the pressure of the breath, or the length of the tube. The shorter the tube, or 'air column' the higher the note. Recorders and flutes have holes along the tube that alter the length of the tube when they are covered or uncovered. With trumpets, the valves alter the length of the tube. Wind instruments are divided into two main groups, woodwind and brass, according to the material from which they were originally made. Confusingly, though, some woodwind instruments, such as the flute saxophone, are made of metal – and even brass.

☑ THE FALL OF JERICHO
The trumpet is one of the oldest wind instruments. According to the Bible, the city of Jericho was defeated when the Israelites sounded their trumpets, causing the city walls to collapse. This would have taken place in about 1200 BC. The first trumpets (and horns) were plain tubes. A player adjusted the sound with lips and tongue.

▱ SOUSAPHONE
The bigger a wind instrument, the deeper the sound it will make. One of the biggest is the tuba, played in orchestras and brass bands to give a rich tone to the music. The sousaphone is a kind of tuba used in marching bands. It is named after the American composer of marching tunes John Sousa (1854–1932).

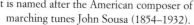

◩ LOUIS ARMSTRONG

Jazz music is often played on wind instruments. One of the most famous jazz musicians was the American Louis 'Satchmo' Armstrong (1900–71), a gifted trumpet player from New Orleans, the so-called 'birthplace of jazz'.

◩ SNAKE CHARMERS

In North Africa and Asia, some woodwind players are able to make highly poisonous cobras, a type of snake, rear their heads and sway in a kind of dance, as if 'charmed' by the music. In fact, cobras are almost deaf, and are really responding to vibrations in the ground and the swaying movement of the charmer's flute.

◩ REED INSTRUMENTS

Some woodwind instruments, such as the clarinet, have 'reeds'– thin strips of cane or metal that set up vibrations inside the instrument. A clarinet's reed is in the mouthpiece.

THE SERPENT

The serpent was a deep-sounding trumpet. It was used to play military and church music for about 400 years, until the 1800s. Its shape allowed the player to reach the holes far down the tube, which may be over 1.8 metres long.

◩ SCOTTISH BAGPIPES

Scottish bagpipes are woodwind instruments with a reed. Like a flute or a recorder, they have a tube with holes in, but instead of blowing directly into this, the player blows through another tube into a bag, where the air is stored. It is squeezed out again by the arm into the tube with holes – the 'chanter'. The bag also plays a continuous background sound through a set of drone pipes at the top of the instrument.

Stringed instruments

PLUCKING a taut rubber band produces a twanging sound, and the range of notes varies if the rubber band is stretched. This is also the principle of stringed instruments. Strings at various tensions are plucked, rubbed or struck to make them vibrate. A sound box amplifies the vibrations, making them louder. The shape of the sound box helps to improve the quality of the sound, making it richer and more rounded. Generally, the larger the sound box, the deeper and louder the sound.

◲ GREEK LYRE

The ancient Greeks played a harplike stringed instrument called a lyre, like the one shown on this Greek vase. But even older pictures show that lyres were used in Mesopotamia about 3000 BC. A lyre has two distinctive curved arms attached to a crossbar and a sound box.

◪ DULCIMER

The dulcimer has strings of different lengths stretched across a flat sound box. The player strikes the strings using a pair of flattened sticks, making a bright, ringing sound. Originating in the Middle East, the dulcimer was popular in Europe from the 1600s to the 1800s. The zither is similar, but its strings are plucked with the fingers.

◳ MARIACHI

A violin is played by drawing a bow across the four strings. In Mexico, groups of up to twelve musicians called mariachis play lively, popular songs on violins, guitars, double basses, harps and sometimes trumpets. They often play at weddings or simply in the street, where passers-by pay them a few dollars to play their favourite song.

◁ DOUBLE BASS

The giant of the violin family is the double bass. Its four thick strings can be plucked or played with a bow. The deep sounds are amplified by the huge wooden sound box. The double bass is played in orchestras and often forms part of jazz bands.

▢ SITAR OF INDIA

The great instrument of classical Indian music is the sitar. It has two sets of strings: one to play the melody, the other to set up a background vibration, giving the instrument its distinctive sound. The left hand presses, or 'stops' the strings to make different notes, while the right hand plucks them.

▢ JAPANESE KOTO

The koto is a kind of zither, played on the floor. The 13 silk strings are stretched over a wooden sound box measuring nearly 1.8 metres long. They are plucked with three plectrums, which are like nail extensions, worn on the right hand, while the left hand adjusts the notes. Each string is raised above the sound box on its own bridge, which can be moved to make different notes.

GUITAR

The guitar came to Europe in medieval times. It has had six strings since the 1600s. Different notes are made by pressing the strings over frets on the fingerboard, and strumming or plucking them with the other hand.

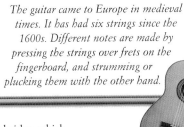

MUSIC

Keyboard instruments

COMPARED to percussion, wind and stringed instruments, keyboard instruments are a fairly recent invention, dating back only about a thousand years. Through a set of levers inside the instrument, each key can produce a precise note – all the player has to do is press the key. The kind of sound that results depends on the instrument. With a piano, the keys trigger hammers that strike a set of tuned strings. With an organ, the keys release air into a set of organ pipes, each sounding a different note. The advantage of keyboard instruments is that you can use all ten fingers (and even your feet) at the same time, and so produce a rich musical effect from a single instrument.

◪ CLAVICHORD

The clavichord was one of the first keyboard instruments. It was developed in the 1300s. Each key acted like a seesaw. When pressed, the other end rose up to hit one of the strings, which were arranged over a sound box, rather like a dulcimer.

◰ CHURCH ORGAN

The first keyboards were made for organs, but the keys were huge and had to be operated with a fist. Finger-sized keyboards were introduced in the 1300s. Keys, foot pedals, and knobs called 'stops' operate the flow of air into the organ pipes. Each pipe is tuned to one note. This church organ is in Naples, Italy.

◪ ELECTRIC ORGAN

Electronic keyboard instruments work on the same principle as organs and pianos, but the sounds are produced by electrical currents, and then amplified in a loud-speaker. The sound can be adjusted electronically to make a very wide range of sounds, imitating all kinds of different instruments, including drums.

◪ HARPSICHORD

While the earlier clavichord had to be set on a table, the harpsichord had its own legs. It developed after the 1500s through other similar instruments such as the virginal and spinet. The big difference with all these is that the strings are not struck, but plucked by a plectrum or 'jack' which is pushed past the string when a key is pressed. Harpsichords were very popular in the 18th century. Mozart learned to play the harpsichord as a child, astounding admiring audiences as he toured Europe from the age of six.

KEYBOARD SINGER

One advantage of the keyboard is that players can accompany themselves as they sing. This is why many songwriters – like the former Beatle Paul McCartney (b. 1942) – use the piano both to compose and to perform.

◪ PLAYING THE PIANO

The full name of the piano is pianoforte, which means 'soft-loud' in Italian. It is so-called because it can be played loudly or softly, by altering pressure on the keys and by using the foot pedals. Invented in the early 1700s, the piano soon became more popular than the harpsichord, which gave players little opportunity to add 'expression' to their playing. Unlike the harpsichord, a piano's strings are not plucked, but struck with a 'hammer'. The metal strings are stretched across a massive metal frame, which may be set flat, as in a grand piano, or vertically, as in the more common upright piano. The hammers are operated by a system of levers attached to the keys.

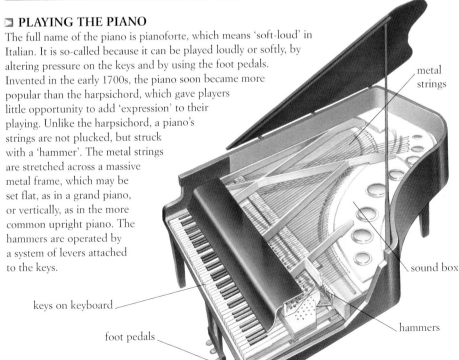

metal strings

sound box

keys on keyboard

foot pedals

hammers

Hybrid instruments

INSTRUMENTS are generally classed as belonging to one of three main categories: percussion, stringed, or wind. But some instruments, such as the saxophone, incorporate elements from more than one category (they are called hybrid instruments). Hybrids are the result of musicians and instrument makers trying to produce new kinds of sounds. Some inventions never really caught on, like the tromba marina, or 'sea trumpet' of the 17th century – a vast cello-like instrument whose one string produced a weird, trumpet-like sound.

For his opera *The Magic Flute* (1791), the German composer Mozart used a mechanical glockenspiel, a kind of keyboard-operated xylophone, the exact details of which have been lost.

◪ SAXOPHONE

One of the most popular wind instruments is the saxophone, or 'sax' which was invented in 1845. Although made of brass, it is classed as a woodwind instrument because it has a reed like a clarinet, and keys like an oboe or flute.

◪ ONDES MARTENOT

One of the earliest electronic instruments was invented in 1928 by the French inventor Maurice Martenot (1898–1980). It was also called an *ondes musicales*, meaning 'musical waves' in French. Played on a keyboard, the loudspeaker produces a great range of haunting sounds. Several major composers wrote music for it.

◪ ONE-MAN BAND

The ultimate hybrid instrument is a one man band. Using pedals, straps, and harnesses, a single musician can perform feats of great physical coordination, using hands, feet and mouth all at once to produce the sound of a mini-orchestra.

◁ MINIATURE ORGAN

An accordion is a kind of miniature organ that can be carried around. With it strapped to the chest, a player uses both hands to stretch it open and squeeze it closed, forcing air past the reeds and making them vibrate. A tune is played using both hands, pressing the keys on one side and the buttons on the other. It was invented in 1822, about the same time as the concertina.

HURDY-GURDY

A hurdy-gurdy is a kind of mechanical violin. However, the strings are not played with a bow, but by a wheel turned with a handle. And instead of making notes by 'stopping' the strings on a fingerboard, the player presses the keys on a tiny keyboard set next to the strings. Both Mozart and Haydn wrote music for the hurdy-gurdy.

◁ CARILLON BELLS

During medieval times, towns in the Netherlands, Belgium and Germany built towers with large bells in them to ring out the time and sound the alarm in the event of an emergency. The sets of bells became very elaborate, and had keyboards attached to them for playing tunes. This 20th-century carillon at the Zwinger Palace of Dresden, Germany, has a carillon of 40 bells made of the fine china called porcelain.

◁ GLASS HARMONICA

If you run a wet finger around the rim of a glass, you may be able to produce a rather beautiful, eerie humming sound. This principle, and earlier instruments based on it, inspired the American statesman Benjamin Franklin (1706–90) to create the glass harmonica. It was popular for a time, and both Beethoven and Mozart wrote music for it.

Voice

THE simplest and most natural of all musical instruments is the human voice. We can assume that people have been singing since the beginning of human history. Pictures from the past, for example from ancient Egypt, are believed to show singers, but we can only guess what kind of sound they made. The human voice is like a musical instrument. The vocal cords set up vibrations, which are amplified in the chest, throat, mouth and nose. Professional singers have to have natural gifts such as an ability to sing in tune and with an attractive sound, but they may also need years of specialized training.

◤ SINGING TOGETHER

A number of people singing together in a choir can produce a rich sound, especially if the choir contains various types of voices, each singing a slightly different tune or 'part'. Choirs developed their skills in churches, but later began singing concerts, like this 18th-century Orphans' Choir in Venice.

◤ ELTON JOHN

Singers are among the richest and most successful people in the modern music world – especially if they write their own songs. The British singer-songwriter and pianist Elton John (b. 1947) has had numerous hits since his first in 1970. His song 'Candle in the Wind', sung at the funeral of Princess Diana, sold 35 million copies, making it an all-time top-selling single.

◣ THE THREE TENORS

In 1990, an operatic song, or aria, was chosen as the theme tune for the soccer World Cup. 'Nessun Dorma' from the opera *Turandot* by Giacomo Puccini (1858–1924), was sung by the three great tenors Placido Domingo, José Carreras and Luciano Pavarotti, and became a worldwide hit.

◪ MUSICAL PLAYS

Singing is a central feature of musicals, a more popular kind of stage play than opera, in which all the words are sung.

Musicals often contain songs that become hits. One of the leading writers of musicals is Andrew Lloyd Webber (b. 1948). His musical *Cats* was first performed in 1981, and holds the record for the longest-running musical both in London and New York.

BALLAD SINGERS

Ballads are traditional songs that tell a story, often about the adventures of ordinary people. They were usually sung by one or two people, perhaps with guitars. Printed copies of the songs were often sold in the street.

◪ SINGING AND TALKING

When African-American DJs in New York began half-singing, half-talking to dance music in the late 1970s, they launched 'rap'. Rap started as a rhyming commentary about daily life in the city, and the music was put together by 'sampling' excerpts of other records. Still popular, it is performed by current top American artists such as Ice T.

◪ GOSPEL MUSIC

When African slaves in the United States converted to Christianity in the 19th century, they brought their own kind of rhythms to the hymns that they sang in church. A distinctive 'gospel music' developed – a joyful, energetic sound in praise of God, full of passion and emotion, and often accompanied by swaying and hand clapping.

Playing together

SINGLE – or solo – musicians can make an attractive sound on their own. But by playing with other musicians they can make a richer and more intricate sound. Groups of musicians have been playing together since the start of music, developing traditions and styles that have been passed down from one generation to the next. Most countries in the world have developed their own distinctive music. An Indonesian gamelan orchestra, for example, is utterly different from a Western chamber orchestra, and its music is just as complex.

◪ EGYPTIAN MUSIC

In the tomb of a royal scribe in ancient Egypt, wall paintings from about 1360 BC show a group of musicians playing for dancers. Such groups may have included pipes, flutes, harps and drums. Dancers sometimes played tambourines.

◩ GREAT COMPOSER

In the past, dancers at balls were accompanied by orchestras like this one. One of the greatest composers of dance music was the Austrian Johann Strauss (1825–99), who wrote a large number of famous waltzes, including 'The Blue Danube'.

◪ ORCHESTRA

Since the 19th century, large-scale classical music has been played by symphony orchestras with about 100 musicians. To make a balanced sound, the musicians are grouped in sections, usually with the strings at the front, woodwind and then brass behind, and percussion at the back. Composers can choose to use more or fewer musicians, or add instruments such as harps.

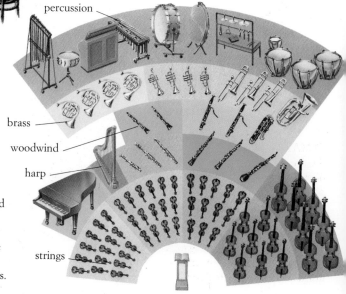

percussion

brass

woodwind

harp

strings

CONDUCTOR

The job of the conductor is to rehearse and direct the musicians. He or she shows them the speed and rhythm (often using a baton), and how to obtain the right balance in sound.

◻ JAZZ BAND

The exciting rhythms of jazz became hugely popular in the 1920s. Joe 'King' Oliver and his Creole Jazz Band, from Chicago, formed one of the most famous groups. Jazz bands of the time often included drums, strings and a piano.

◻ FOLK BAND

Folk dance music is usually played by small bands of about five or so players, as with this band in Lithuania. They play traditional tunes, dating back perhaps hundreds of years. The type of music that they play, as well as the traditional costumes of the dancers, is often closely associated with national identity.

◻ MARCHING BAND

Soldiers marching to war were often accompanied by bands that played tunes to lift their spirits and help them to march in step. The bands consisted entirely of wind and percussion instruments. Most modern marching bands have nothing to do with the army, but they use the same kinds of instruments and wear uniforms.

Composers

ALL music has to be created, or composed, by
someone. A large proportion of traditional
music was created hundreds of years ago by
unknown composers, and passed down from one
generation to the next, being altered and perhaps
improved at each stage. In Europe, composers
developed the practice of writing down music.
As a result, we know the names of the composers,
and also more or less how they wanted the music
to sound. Many Western composers developed the
ability to write complex music straight onto the
page by first imagining the
sounds in their heads. They
could then give the music
to an orchestra to play.

 **WRITTEN MUSIC**
In medieval times, composers
devised a kind of visual
picture of sounds, so that they
could be read by others. It was
based on the musical scale –
the progression of notes from
lowest to highest, as played on
an instrument. Each note in
the scale was given a position
on a set of horizontal lines. By
reading the written music
from left to right, musicians
could see the order in which
to play the notes.

◄ MONTEVERDI
The Italian composer
Claudio Monteverdi
(1567–1643) became famous
for his church music. He also
wrote one of the first operas,
Orfeo, in 1607. Although
Monteverdi lived and worked
in and around Venice, his fame
spread because he was able to
publish his work in printed form.

◪ COMPOSING MUSIC
When creating a complicated
piece of work for many
instruments, composers often
try out their ideas on a piano.
One of the greatest-ever
composers, the German Ludwig
van Beethoven (1770–1827),
worked in this way. In sketch
books, he wrote down the music
that he wanted each instrument
to play, before taking it to the
orchestra to try out.

THE SCORE – PRINTED MUSIC

The written or printed music that an orchestra plays from is called the 'score'. It shows all the parts that the different instruments play and how they fit together. This is part of the handwritten score of the opera *The Barber of Seville* by the Italian composer Gioachino Rossini (1782–1868).

YOUNG COMPOSER

Wolfgang Amadeus Mozart (1756–91) was one of the greatest composers of Western music. Born and brought up in Austria, he was a child prodigy who began composing at the age of five, and went on to write church music, concertos, symphonies, and operas. He composed entire works in his head and wrote them straight onto the page. Mozart led a very full life in Salzburg and Vienna, and died aged just 35.

MUSICAL NOTES

Written notes (or notation) do not simply show their 'pitch' – how high and low they are. They also show how long they should be played for. Notes range in length from a whole note (or semi-breve) which is played for four beats, to a sixteenth note (or semi-quaver), which lasts for a quarter of a beat.

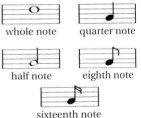

whole note   quarter note

half note   eighth note

sixteenth note

COMPUTER COMPOSITION

Max Mathews was a pioneer of computer music. In 1963 he helped to devise a way of 'synthesizing' musical sounds into a digital form that could be stored in a computer and played back. Computers can store vast quantities of sound information, and so can imitate all kinds of instruments, and even styles of playing them.

Classical music

WESTERN classical music grew first out of church music. The search for an ever more complex and rich sound led to improved standards of instrument making. This would not have been possible without patrons – rich people who paid composers to write new music, and paid musicians to perform it. During the 15th century, kings and nobles also became important patrons of fine music. Classical music developed further because composers could write down their music, and then have it printed – so orchestras anywhere could play it, even if the composer was not present. Orchestras try to play the music accurately, but also to 'interpret' it, giving it their own individual character and feeling.

◪ **BEETHOVEN**
Ludwig van Beethoven (1720–1827) was the most brilliant pianist of his day. He played with great passion – a passion that is also found in his many compositions. The traditional orchestra had to be enlarged to play his complex symphonies, which were considered extremely modern at the time.

◨ **SCHOENBERG**
The Austrian composer Arnold Schoenberg (1874–1951) was a pioneer of modern music. He abandoned the traditional harmonies of the eight-note scale, and instead worked with all the notes, producing an entirely new sound called 'atonal music'.

◨ **OPERA**
Opera began as a kind of musical entertainment, combining music, singing and dance. Gradually it developed into the form it has today, a full play in which the entire story is sung to classical music. Shown here is a performance of *Aida*, a tragic story set in ancient Egypt, by the great opera composer Giuseppe Verdi (1813–1901).

◻ BALLET

Classical music has been written specially for ballet. *Swan Lake*, for example – for which this is a costume – was written by the great Russian composer Pyott Ilíyich Tchaikovsky (1840–93). It was first performed at the Bolshoi Theatre in Moscow in 1877. Tchaikovsky also wrote the music for operas and symphonies.

◻ HANDEL

George Frideric Handel (1685– 1759) was a German composer and a gifted musician, playing violin and harpsichord. He came to England in 1712 and worked for Queen Anne and King George I. One of his most popular works is *Music for the Royal Fireworks,* designed to be played outdoors with a firework display.

STRAVINSKY

Some of the most exciting ballet of the 20th century was performed by the Russian company the Ballets Russes, led by Sergei Diaghilev. He commissioned a number of composers to create music for them. One of these was Igor Stravinsky (1882–1971), who wrote Firebird, Petrushka *and* The Rite of Spring, *and became one of the greatest composers of the 20th century.*

◻ CLASSICAL MUSIC TODAY

A few years ago, many people thought that classical music had lost its popular appeal. But with the help of CDs, TV exposure and classical music radio stations, a new generation of talented and glamorous performers like Vanessa Mae (b. 1979) have found a new audience, and demonstrated that classical music is very much alive.

Improvisation

SOME kinds of music are not bound to a written score. Instead, the musicians are free to play what they like and express their own emotions, although they usually start and end with a recognizable theme. This kind is called 'improvisation'. It is most closely associated with jazz music. In a famous piece of jazz, for instance, the American saxophonist John Coltrane played his own highly original version of 'My Favourite Things' from the popular musical *The Sound of Music*. But many other kinds of music also involve improvisation, such as blues, rock, Indian sitar music and traditional dance music.

◪ STÉPHANE GRAPPELLI

The French jazz musician Stéphane Grappelli (1908–97) played the violin in an utterly original way, at great speed and with a highly individual style of improvisation. In the 1930s he played with the great jazz guitarist Django Reinhardt (1910–53).

◪ PLAYING THE SAXOPHONE

John Coltrane (1926–67) was one of the greatest American jazz musicians. He played tenor saxophone with some of the top bands of his day, such those led by Dizzie Gillespie (1917–93) and Miles Davis (1926–91), before forming his own quartet. His innovative music laid many of the foundations of modern jazz.

◪ ELVIS PRESLEY

In the 1950s, young white American musicians started to produce upbeat guitar music based on 'country-and-western' and black 'rhythm and blues'. It was called 'rock 'n' roll' and the 'King' was Elvis Presley (1935–77). At first he was thought of as a rebel, but he went on to sing many songs that have become classic hits.

◁ DIXIELAND, SWING AND BEBOP

Jazz developed in New Orleans in about 1900. 'Dixieland' jazz created a fun, raucous sound based on popular songs. In the 1930s and 1940s jazz musicians in big bands created the smoother, plusher dance sound of 'swing'. The faster, more rhythmic 'bebop' jazz was introduced by smaller groups in the late 1940s. One of the key musicians in this movement was the alto sax player Charlie 'Bird' Parker (1920–55), seen on the right here playing in New York in 1949.

◁ ROCK MUSIC

In the late 1960s, bands started to mix rock 'n' roll, jazz and blues, amplified it electronically and created the style now known as 'rock'. The Irish group U2 emerged as one of the leading rock bands in the 1980s, fronted by the singer Bono (Paul Hewson, b. 1960). U2 was hugely popular in both Britain and America.

WURLITZER ORGAN

Before 1927, movies had no soundtrack. Instead the 'silent movies' were accompanied by musicians who watched the film and made up music to mirror the action. In 1911 a US organ-making company called Wurlitzer began producing elaborate cinema organs that could make a wide range of orchestral sounds and sound effects.

◁ RHYTHM AND BLUES

The blues is a type of heartfelt folk music that was originally sung by African slaves in the southern states of America. It has played a key role in the development of modern popular music. In the 1940s it reached a wider audience through a fusion with jazz, called 'rhythm and blues' (or R & B). One of the best-known R & B musicians was the guitarist B. B. King (b. 1925), a great promoter of the blues.

Recorded music

THE development of sound-recording devices has transformed the way we listen to music. Before the invention of the first gramophones, the only way to hear music was to see it played live – or to play it oneself. But gramophones made it possible to hear top performers and music from other parts of the world, without leaving home. The spread of radio in the 1920s had a similar effect. Today, most of the music we listen to is recorded music. With digital technology the quality of recorded music has become exceptionally good – better, often, than live music. But many people argue that live performances still convey more of a sense of inspiration and emotion than recorded music ever can.

◪ SOUND RECORDING

The first gramophone, called a phonograph, was produced by the American inventor Thomas Alva Edison in 1878. It used cylinders to record and play sounds. Ten years later the first flat disc was introduced. A needle picked up the sound from grooves in the disc.

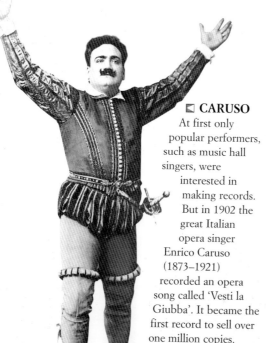

◪ CARUSO

At first only popular performers, such as music hall singers, were interested in making records. But in 1902 the great Italian opera singer Enrico Caruso (1873–1921) recorded an opera song called 'Vesti la Giubba'. It became the first record to sell over one million copies. Ever since, classical musicians have made recordings.

◪ RADIO ENTERTAINMENT

The radio was invented by the Italian Guglielmo Marconi in 1894. At first it was designed only to transmit simple messages, but in 1906 music was broadcast. By the time this picture was taken in the 1940s, many households in Europe and America had a radio. It was the most popular form of family entertainment before the arrival of television in the 1950s.

◪ RECORDING STUDIO

In a modern recording studio, electronic equipment records sounds on a number of tracks, often one instrument at a time. The sound engineers can alter the tracks, by changing the pitch, for example, or adding new sounds. Then they 'mix' all the tracks together and carefully adjust the balance between the tracks to produce a finished recording.

◪ QUEEN OF POP

Ever since her hit single 'Holiday' in 1984, the American singer and songwriter Madonna (Madonna Louise Ciccone, b. 1958) has been a top recording artist. She has had 35 top-ten hits, and 50 of her records have sold over a million copies. A master of publicity, she continually alters her image through her pop videos.

◪ JUKE BOX

In the days when records were produced on plastic or vinyl discs (from the late 1940s to the 1990s), they came in two forms: LPs (long-playing) and 45s (smaller records that revolved faster, at 45 revolutions per minute). The top-ten charts were based entirely on 'singles' which came on 45s. In places like bars, cafés and youth clubs, a selection of 45s was put into a machine called a juke box. Listeners put money in the slot, selected the record they wanted to hear, and the machine played it for them.

CD

The trouble with vinyl discs was that they could be easily damaged by scratching. In the 1990s a new kind of record began to replace vinyl. Compact discs (CDs) were not only neater and more solid: their digital and laser technology offered a more accurate recording, and a better sound quality.

The music industry

IN the days before recorded music, composers, and music publishers made money by printing and selling sheet music. Now, with CDs, cassettes, pop videos, and more recently the Internet, music publishing has become a multi-million-dollar international industry. The top stars of popular music sell millions of copies of their recordings all over the world, and because they earn a percentage of the sale price as a 'royalty', they can earn vast sums of money. There is considerable skill in spotting, promoting and nurturing talent. In the pop music business, musical talent may be less important than youth and personality. But classical music still demands very high standards of musicianship.

◪ CLASSICAL STAR

One of the most fascinating stars of classical music was the Italian violinist and composer Niccolo Paganini (1782–1840). He was a 'virtuoso' – a player with dazzling gifts – who could play extremely complex pieces, and at such great speed that some people suggested he must be in league with the Devil.

◪ PAUL ROBESON

Many people came to know the American Paul Robeson (1898–1976) through his recorded music, and he became one of the most important black singers of his time, famous for his rich, bass voice. Robeson was a theatre and screen actor as well as a singer. He first made his name internationally in a tour of the stage musical *Show Boat* in 1928, in which he sang his best-known song 'Ol' Man River'.

◰ MUSIC SHOP

Since the early history of music, instrument makers have played a vital role in the music business. The better the quality of an instrument, the better the sound it makes, and usually the more it costs. Good music shops offer a wide selection of instruments for players to try out.

◨ SPICE WORLD

A feature of modern pop music is the girl band or boy band. Producers in the music industry select a group of young and glamorous singers, find suitable songs for them, and then launch them in a blaze of publicity. The Spice Girls were an immediate success in 1996, and had number-one hits with their first three singles.

THE BEATLES

The world's most successful recording group of the 1960s was the British band the Beatles. The 'Fab Four' were Paul McCartney (b. 1942), John Lennon (1940–80), George Harrison (1943–2002), and Ringo Starr (b. 1940).

◨ INVENTIVE SONGWRITER

In the late 1960s, there was a sharp division between pop and rock music. People tended to like one and hate the other. During the early 1970s, the gap was closed by inventive songwriters like British singer David Bowie (b. 1947), who was also famous for his extravagant stage performances.

◨ HUGE SUCCESS

One of the most successful 'boy bands' of the 1990s was the American group the Backstreet Boys. All talented singers, they formed in 1992 and became stars first in Europe and Canada. Their breakthrough at home came in 1997 with their album Backstreet Boys, which sold 13 million copies.

M
U
S
I
C

World music

LIKE many other industries, the music business has become global. One advantage of this is that all kinds of musical styles from around the world are now being recorded, listened to and studied. Such styles range from traditional music, whose patterns have not changed for hundreds of years, to modern hybrid forms of music – a blend of local traditional music with modern electronic pop. Popular music today may show influences of South American dance music, North African singing, Indian tabla rhythms, or Indonesian gamelan. Music is always changing and developing, and today the mix is becoming richer and more complex than ever.

◢ INUIT DRUM DANCE
The Inuit of Canada and Greenland perform a traditional dance to the beat of a large, caribou-skin drum (a *qilaut*). Individual men take turns to play the drum and dance, accompanied by singing. The dances often act out a story, told in the singing, usually about hunting or animals.

◤ SOUTH AFRICAN SINGER
Black South Africa has a rich tradition in music. One of the first singers to demonstrate this to the world was Miriam Makeba (b. 1932), who moved to the United States in the 1960s to escape the harsh apartheid regime. Combining music with political activities, she recorded many Xhosa and Zulu songs. She returned to South Africa in 1990.

◣ MUSIC FOR THE WORLD
An important development in the promotion of world music was the creation of WOMAD (World of Music, Arts and Dance), which held its first festival in 1982. Since then there have been more than 90 festivals and events in 20 countries, featuring musicians from all over the world.

INDIAN FOLK MUSIC

Bhangra is the name of a type of folk dance in Punjab, a region bordering north India and Pakistan. This acrobatic and colourful dance is performed to celebrate the harvest. In the 1980s, the Asian community in Britain developed a modern dance music with the same name, blending traditional Indian music with electronic instruments, drum machines, reggae and disco music.

PAUL SIMON – SINGER-SONGWRITER

The American singer-songwriter Paul Simon (b. 1941) became famous in the 1960s and 1970s as half of the duo Simon and Garfunkel (with Art Garfunkel, b. 1941). In 1986 he worked with musicians from the South African townships, such as the Ladysmith Black Mambazo, to produce Graceland, a hugely successful record album and tour. He continues to explore the fusion between Western, African, and South American music.

REGGAE MUSIC

Reggae is a type of dance music from Jamaica, noted for its use of a heavy, offbeat rhythm. It was made world-famous in the 1970s by Bob Marley (1945–81) and his group The Wailers. After 'No Woman, No Cry' (1975), he had a string of hits, until his early death from cancer. Reggae was one of the first non-American music styles to have a major impact on pop music.

RAVI SHANKAR

'The Godfather of World Music' is how the great Indian sitar player Ravi Shankar (b. 1920) has been described. He has been playing his music around the world since 1954. Not only is he a supreme performer of Indian classical music, but he has also studied ways of mixing it with Western classical music.

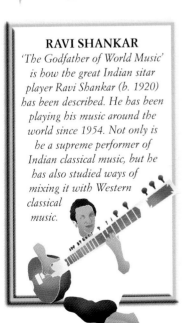

Design

OBJECTS that are planned and made for a particular purpose are described as being 'designed'. The word is most frequently used in connection with fashion, architecture, computers and publishing. But design also forms an important part of most manufacturing and engineering processes. A designer combines problem-solving with creativity and precise attention to detail. Today, the word 'designer' is often used to suggest that items are of good quality, and in the latest, exclusive style. But in the past, there were many discussions and disagreements about what made 'good' design.

Many kinds of design

WE ARE surrounded by examples of 'design'. But they often have very different origins. Some are so old that we do not know who invented them. They have changed in detail over thousands of years, but their essential structure and function is the same. Others are based on old ideas, but have been modified by the discovery of new materials, or scientific techniques. Some exclusive designs are still handmade in traditional style. For the past 200 years, many designs have been shaped by the processes used to make them. Today, most designed items combine cheapness of manufacture with popular mass-market appeal.

◿ NATIONAL SYMBOL

Currency notes are designed as a sign of national identity, and, often, pride. They are decorated with easily recognizable national symbols such as portraits of national heroes or famous landmarks.

◿ USEFUL OR BEAUTIFUL?

For centuries, people have questioned whether a well-designed object is simply one that is good to look at, or whether it should be practical as well. Traditional blacksmiths tried to combine usefulness with attractive designs when making simple tools and iron fastenings.

◿ HIGH RISE

The first 'skyscrapers' were built in the late 19th century. Originally they were designed to make the best use of limited space at ground level, as well as to look impressive. But critics claim that skyscrapers can be lonely places in which to live, and that they cause 'visual pollution'.

OLD OR NEW?

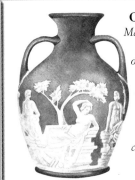

Many designers strive to be original, while others borrow from the past. In the 18th and 19th centuries, British vase designers were influenced by the art of ancient Rome, creating similar styles of their own.

☑ INDIVIDUAL STYLE

Some designers win fame for their personal style. The Spanish architect Antonio Gaudi (1853–1926) is famous for his original and unusual building designs. Most of his buildings are in the city of Barcelona in Spain. In an attempt to break away from historical styles, he used flowing curves in many of his buildings, which he decorated with brightly coloured ceramics or mosaics of glass.

▧ MASS-PRODUCED

From the 19th century onward, millions of identical items were made by machines in factories. Mass-production allowed people to buy attractive, practical goods more cheaply than ever before. Before mass-production, tools, clothes, furniture and household items were all made slowly and carefully by hand, and were often very expensive.

☑ SAFETY FIRST

Bridges are some of the biggest and most beautiful structures in the world. But their graceful curves and arches are the result of careful mathematical calculations, not simply 'artistic' design. Their strength and safety are more important than their appearance.

Who designs?

EVERYTHING that is made – by hand or by machine – is the result of a decision. Someone, somewhere, has decided to paint, carve, sew, assemble or construct it using particular materials and a specific plan. Some objects are the result of long years of tradition. Their original shape, size, or component parts may have been adapted or improved over the centuries. More recent objects are often created either as experiments, to set fashion trends, to meet an urgent need or just for fun. The designers' names are generally known, and they may even be celebrities, particularly if they design clothes.

◖ FAMOUS ARTISTS

For thousands of years, artists have been employed to create beautiful paintings and sculptures to bring glory to rich nations or powerful families. This stone carving was made by Phidias, the most famous sculptor in ancient Greece, about 430 BC. It decorated the Parthenon, a splendid temple in Athens.

◤ TOOLS FOR THE JOB

One of the earliest-designed tools was the stone axe, made for cutting. This one was made about 8000 BC. Stone axes helped bring about a revolution in food production. The earliest farmers used them to chop down trees and clear land so they could grow crops.

◤ DESIGNED BY SCRIBES

Ancient Egypt's pyramids, the giant tombs of the pharaohs (kings), were designed by scribes – well-educated writers from each pharaoh's court. They were built by people who normally farmed the land.

MASTER MASONS
During the Middle Ages (c. AD 1000–1500), master masons designed and built magnificent cathedrals in many European cities. On the plaster floors of their 'drawing-rooms' they drew detailed plans for stone windows and arches.

◧ SKILL AND CALCULATION
Design is often a matter of artistic flair combined with rigorous mechanical calculation. Both are essential to create an object that looks good and functions well. Great sailing ships, like these shown in an 18th-century dockyard, looked beautiful. But their design was also carefully calculated to keep them afloat, carry loads and sail fast.

▣ LIVING IN STYLE
People have always liked their surroundings to reflect their artistic tastes and sense of style. Some pay for experts, called 'interior designers' to design their homes. Others consult books, magazines and TV programmes for new decorative ideas. This design for a family drawing room was published in a British magazine in 1884.

◧ DESIGNS FOR KNOWLEDGE
During the late 20th century, designers emerged in the new field of 'information technology' (IT). Some specialized in electronics, telecommunications or computer hardware. Others created web sites with sounds and moving pictures, or devised specialized software for scientists like this oceanographer.

DESIGN

Houses and furnishings

ALL around the word, people's basic housing needs are the same. They want a home that will provide shelter from heat or cold, somewhere comfortable to eat and sleep, and protection from intruders or enemies. Many different designs have developed to meet these needs. Today's homes are often built from factory-made materials such as concrete, plastic, steel and tinted glass. In the past, builders had to use local supplies of materials such as wood, clay or stone, as it was too difficult – and costly – to transport them long distances. Home furnishings are often status symbols. Rich people may choose exclusive, luxurious designs as a sign of wealth and power. Poor people have to survive in much smaller, often crowed homes that may not have clean water, heating or power supplies.

◣ MALI MOUNTAIN HOMES
The Dogon people of Mali, in Africa, design their villages in the shape of the first woman created by God, to reflect their religious beliefs. The men's meeting house is her head, groups of family homes are her body, and women's private rooms are her hands.

◪ FAMILY VALUES
In 1895, the sitting room of a moderately wealthy family in America was designed to provide a comfortable living space for a large number of people. Painting, reading, sewing, letter writing and conversation were usual pastimes, but everything was kept neat and tidy, reflecting the shared family values.

◩ OLD AND NEW
Ideas about design change rapidly over time. They change with fashion, developing technology, and with new ideas about the best way to live. Big cities often reveal great contrasts between old and new housing designs. In Singapore, for example, these traditional low-rise, decorated houses are dwarfed by modern high-rise apartments.

☑ MODERN LIVING

In the late 20th century, kitchens were filled with all kinds of functional, but unattractive, electric-powered devices such as refrigerators, dishwashers and microwave ovens. Homeowners concealed them in specially designed, matching cupboards like these. Today, many appliances have become 'designer' items, and the fashion is to display them.

FOREST HOMES
Traditionally, Scandinavian homes like this Swedish house were built of pine wood from the nearby forests. Furniture, tools and utensils were also made of pine, often painted with bright designs.

☐ FOR CITY MERCHANTS

In crowded cities, where there is not much space for building, houses are often built several storeys high and closely packed together, to fit in as many people as possible. These tall merchants' houses in Amsterdam, in the Netherlands, were designed about 1650. They were built beside one of the city's many canals, which were used by cargo boats. Some houses had cranes in the roof to haul goods up to attic store rooms. Today, waterside houses are often the most desirable, both for homeowners and tourists alike.

◁ UNDER ONE ROOF

In many parts of the world, extended families live together under one roof. On the Southeast Asian island of Sumatra, in Indonesia, for example, the Batak people live in large family groups in decorated wooden houses. The floor of the building is supported on wooden posts at head-height, and is covered by a tall, curved roof that ends in two points, like buffalo horns. Traditionally the houses were held together with wooden pins instead of nails.

Big buildings

WHY do architects design big buildings, and wealthy families or businesses pay for them? Over the centuries there has been one main reason – to impress. Other reasons include political pride and love. Temples and cathedrals were built as places of worship. Arenas were centres for sport. Castles and forts were built to control lords' lands, and great tombs were built as memorials to people who were respected or loved. Public monuments display national pride, while today's huge modern office blocks proclaim a company's – or a city's – wealth, power and confidence.

◩ MYSTERIOUS STONEHENGE
Stonehenge is a massive prehistoric monument in southwest England. The circular bank and ditch, and the three stone circles within them, were built in stages between about 3000 and 1500 BC. No one knows exactly why Stonehenge was built, but it was probably designed as a temple.

◩ THE GREATEST ROMAN AMPHITHEATRE
The Colosseum in Rome, Italy, was the greatest amphitheatre, or circular arena, built by the ancient Romans. It was constructed from an early form of concrete. Completed in AD 80, it was designed to hold 50,000 spectators, who went there to watch bloodthirsty gladiator fights and battles between men and wild animals.

wooden seats for women at the top

tiered seats for men

posts for awning

sand-covered arena

outer corridors

underground cages

◗ MIGHTY CASTLES

Castles were among the biggest buildings in the world before about AD 1800. The earliest castles were built from wood about AD 900, as shelters for soldiers. They developed over the next 300 years into huge stone buildings like this one. More than 20,000 stood in Britain, France and Germany.

TALLEST BUILDINGS

PETRONAS 1 AND 2
Kuala Lumpur, Malaysia
449 metres   1998

SEARS TOWER
Chicago, Illinois
439 metres   1974

JIN MAO BUILDING
Shanghai, China
418 metres   1998

CITIC PLAZA
Guangzhou, China
389 metres   1996

SHUN HING SQUARE
Shenzhen, China
382 metres   1996

EMPIRE STATE BUILDING
New York City
379 metres   1931

CENTRAL PLAZA
Hong Kong
372 metres   1992

BANK OF CHINA
Hong Kong
366 metres   1989

EMIRATES TOWERS
Dubai, UAE
353 metres   1999

THE CENTRE
Hong Kong, CHINA
348 metres   1998

◢ THE EIFFEL TOWER

The 300-metre-high Eiffel Tower in Paris, France, was completed in 1889 to mark the centenary of the French Revolution of 1789. It was made of wrought iron, a new material for structures or buildings at that time.

◣ THE SERENE TAJ MAHAL

The marble Taj Mahal in Agra, India, is one of the largest and most beautiful tombs in the world. Completed about AD 1648, it houses the body of Mumtaz Mahal, wife of Emperor Shah Jahan, who ruled the Mughal empire from 1628 to 1658.

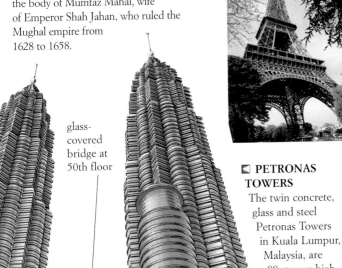

glass-covered bridge at 50th floor

◀ PETRONAS TOWERS

The twin concrete, glass and steel Petronas Towers in Kuala Lumpur, Malaysia, are 88 storeys high and are topped by spires. Each floor is shaped like an eight-pointed star.

Early tools and machines

Humans are the only species on Earth to deliberately design tools and machines to help them with all aspects of their lives. The name 'tool' is usually given to objects designed to perform a specific task, such as hammering or chopping. The word 'machine' is more often used to describe a larger, more complicated object, driven by some kind of motor, rather than human muscle-power. Tools for everyday tasks, such as knives, are usually simple, straightforward and easy to make, as well as easy to use. In contrast, tools and machines for precise purposes, or for tasks that need to be repeated, are often complex in design. Their construction needs special skills.

◪ CUTTING AND DIGGING
About 2.5 million years ago, early humans began to make tools by chipping stones to create a sharp edge. Later Stone Age tools, like this flint hand axe (c.100,000 BC), were designed for cutting up dead animals or digging up edible roots.

◪ LIFTING POWER
Cranes are machines that are designed to lift heavy loads. By 1900, ironworks like this one in Germany were using huge beam cranes to move red-hot iron bars from the furnace to the steam-powered hammer, which hit them into shape.

◪ ANIMAL POWER
For thousands of years, people designed ways of harnessing animal power to help them in their work. Before motorized ploughs were invented, farmers used horse-drawn ploughs to cultivate their fields. Horses wearing padded collars, to cushion the load, were able to pull an iron-tipped plough share through heavy ground.

STEAM ENGINE

Machines powered by steam revolutionized industry in the 19th century. They made all kinds of goods more quickly and cheaply than old-style machines worked by hand. This massive steam engine powered machines in factories in the north of Britain. It was fuelled by coal from the plentiful local mines, and water from the hill streams.

A SCIENTIST'S INSTRUMENT

Tools are used by a person to do a task, whereas instruments provide information. The microscope is an instrument used by scientists to study objects too small to be seen with the naked eye. It was invented in the 17th century. This one was used by Robert Hooke (1635–1703), who first identified cells – the basic building blocks of all living things.

POWER FROM RIVERS AND STREAMS

Water-wheels were probably invented in the Middle East. They have been used for more than 2000 years both to raise water and to harness the power of flowing water to drive machinery. Before the invention of the steam engine in the 1700s, water-wheels were used to power mills, where grain was ground into flour. As water flowed over the paddles on the wheel, it turned the wheel, which then rotated two flat grindstones that crushed the grain.

SCISSORS

Scissors are a cutting tool made from two blades, each with a handle, and joined by a screw in the middle. One handle slips over a finger and the other over the thumb. If the handles are pushed apart, the blades open, and when pulled together, they close with a cutting action. Scissors of bronze or iron were first used in ancient China and Japan, as well as by the Romans. But from 1761, they were cast in steel and mass-produced in England.

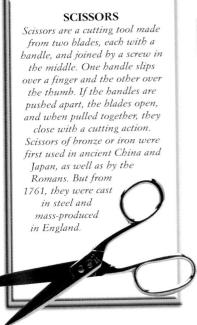

D
E
S
I
G
N

New technologies

FROM about AD 1750, tools and machines were designed by professional scientists, inventors, and engineers. They were made from 'modern' manufactured materials, such as metal alloys (mixtures), in the 19th century, and plastics in the 20th century. Scientific discoveries such as X-rays and jet propulsion allowed inventors to create new technology for medicine, engineering and information handling. Many 21st-century machines no longer need humans to operate them. Instead, they can perform tasks by themselves, and even make simple decisions. Some people predict that, before long, inventors will design a new race of 'cyborgs' – part machine, part human.

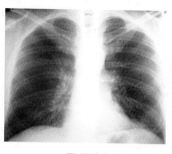

◢ X-RAY VISION
In 1895, X-rays, which allow us to 'see through' substances, were discovered. They are widely used in medicine to diagnose illness, and in engineering to search for hidden cracks and flaws.

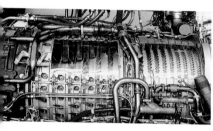

◢ JET-PROPELLED
Jet engines work by compressing and burning oil vapour and air, then pushing out exhaust gases. They were invented in the 1930s by designers Whittle (in Britain) and von Ohain (in Germany). In the late 20th century, aircraft powered by jet engines made air travel quicker and less expensive than ever before.

◣ INSIDE STORY
CAT scanners use X-rays to view 'slices' or cross-sections, of organs inside a person's body. These are presented on a computer screen as digital images for doctors to look at and examine for illness. 'CAT' stands for 'Computerized Axial Tomography' a process first used about 1980.

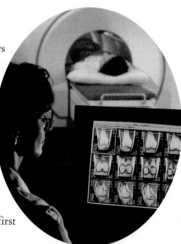

◪ NATURE POWER
Wind power has been used to drive simple machines for centuries, but in the 20th century, engineers invented machines to generate electricity from wind power. Today, many countries, especially in northern Europe, use wind power to generate electricity, instead of making it by burning fossil fuels. It is inexpensive and non-polluting, but noisy.

☑ BLAST OFF!

Rockets were one of the most important machines of the 20th century. Without them, astronauts would not have been able to leave Earth and travel in space. Like jets, rockets are propelled by burning gas. But they also carry a substance called an oxidizer, which allows their engines to operate in space, where there is no air. Simple rockets, fuelled by gunpowder, were made in China about AD 1300. Modern rockets were pioneered by Russian engineer Konstantin Tsiolkovsky (1857–1935). His ideas were later developed in the United States and the former Soviet Union.

COMPUTERS

Computers were originally designed as machines to store and process data. Today, life would be impossible without them for many people. Smaller, and more affordable than ever before, they are used by organizations as diverse as governments and children's play groups.

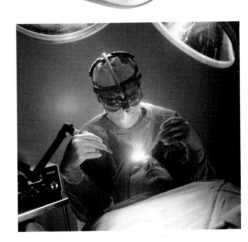

◪ LASER SURGERY

Lasers are machines that produce intense beams of high-energy light. They can melt, burn, or cut through many different substances, from metals to human bodies, and are often used for delicate surgery. They can also be used to make precise measurements, in printing, to guide weapons, and to read supermarket bar codes. Lasers were first built in 1960 by American Theodore Maiman (b. 1927).

DESIGN

Designs for food

FOOD is essential for survival. It can also symbolize love, friendship and happiness. Throughout the past, people have invented ways of cooking raw foodstuffs to make them safe and tasty to eat, and have designed technologies for storing, processing, cooking and serving many different kinds of meat, fish and edible plants. Professional cooks (usually men) and family carers (usually women) have prepared meals to suit many different needs – from fast-food snacks that provide instant body-fuel and satisfy hunger, to elaborate meals that welcome guests and celebrate special occasions.

◀ MAKING OIL

In ancient Greece and Rome, ripe olives were harvested from trees every year and crushed in large wooden presses to extract a rich, fragrant oil. This was used in cooking, cleaning and beauty care, just as it is today.

☑ WELL-TRAINED STAFF

From about AD 1000–1600, wealthy families living in castles employed a large staff of well-trained cooks and kitchen boys, or scullions, to prepare and cook food for them and their guests. Cooking technology was simple. Meat was roasted on spits over huge open fires, or stewed in large metal cauldrons; the basic kitchen tools were knives and spoons.

◤ MADE BY HAND

In the 16th century, Aztec women from Mexico ground maize between stones to make flour and mixed it with water to form dough. They rolled and shaped the dough into tortillas – thin, flat pancakes – and baked them on a heated stone. Tortillas were the Aztecs' basic food.

◪ LOOKING GOOD

Japanese cooks are famous for their skill at arranging food, carefully combining different colours, shapes and textures on the plate. Food that looks good can be a 'feast for the eyes'. Like the smell of good cooking, attractive food increases the appetite and tempts people to eat. Presenting food well also shows respect for the people to whom it is offered.

◪ WELL-PRESERVED

Methods of food preservation were devised hundreds of years ago. People preserved meat and fish by smoking it, drying it or storing it in barrels of salt, as shown here. All three methods kill the bacteria, or germs, that live inside the food. If not preserved, food left at room temperature will begin to decay as the bacteria multiply. Food containing too much harmful bacteria may make people ill, and can even kill them.

COOKING BY RADIO?

Invented in about 1953, microwave ovens use very short radio waves to heat food and cook it. As the radio waves pass through the food, they 'excite' all the molecules of liquid in the food, making the liquid hot. The heat spreads quickly through the food.

◪ CHILLING!

Storing food at low temperatures stops dangerous bacteria from growing, and can keep fruit and vegetables crisp and fresh. Traditionally, food was kept cool in cupboards or small rooms called 'larders'. Refrigerators were invented by American engineer John Gorrie (1803–55) in 1851, and were more reliable. Freezers first appeared in 1929, invented by American businessman Clarence Birdseye (1886–1956). Today, most homes in developed countries have both. Large refrigerated trucks carry chilled or frozen foods from factories direct to the shops to sell.

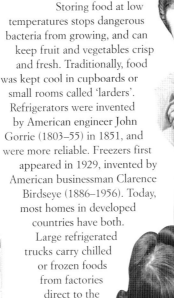

Clothes and fashion

CLOTHES do more than keep us warm. They also display our wealth, status, and, sometimes, our occupation. If they are traditional in style, they may reveal which part of the world we come from, and which faith we follow. If they are unusual, we may wear them as a sign of rebellion, or to show that we belong to a special group. The first clothes ever made were sewn from animal skins and furs about 70,000 years ago. Since then, people have designed clothes, jewellery and make-up in many different styles. Today, designer fashion is big business.

◪ TEXTILE REVOLUTION

The ancient Egyptians wore clothes made of linen, woven from fibres of the flax plant. Long, horizontal looms were used to weave the cloth. About 1500 BC, a new cloth-making technology arrived in Egypt from the Middle East. Expert weavers began to make patterned tapestries from woollen thread on big, upright looms.

◪ BEADS AND FEATHERS

In Papua New Guinea, men attend traditional religious ceremonies wearing face paint and feather headdresses. Ornaments on clothing, traditionally made from feathers, shells and stones, date back over one million years. All over the world, specially designed clothes decorated with extra ornaments are worn for special occasions, such as getting married.

◪ HANDMADE FOOTWEAR

Until the late 19th century, boots, and shoes were made by hand. The cobbler, who was both a shoemaker and mender, cut pieces of leather to make the tops, or uppers, and soles. He fitted these over a foot-shaped model, called a last, and joined them together with stitches or tiny nails.

☑ THE LATEST FASHIONS

Until the 19th century, ordinary people knew little about the new fashions of the rich, or foreign styles. Fashion plates (hand-coloured engravings) spread the news of the latest trends – these dresses were designed in 1883. Paper patterns in magazines and the invention of sewing machines also made fashions more widely available.

COCO CHANEL

Gabrielle 'Coco' Chanel (1883–1971) created a whole new style of clothing for women based on simple designs, often using square shapes. By the 1930s, she was the richest designer in France.

☑ BIG BUSINESS

By the 20th century, designer fashion had become big business. Although world-famous models paraded elegantly down catwalks to display exclusive, handmade garments to wealthy customers, most fashion designers made money from selling cheap, mass-made copies of 'ready-to-wear' collections, or by licensing everyday clothes such as jeans, which were labelled with their names.

☑ BACKSTRAP LOOM

The backstrap loom was invented about 4000 years ago. Lightweight, cheap and portable, it is still used by many peoples around the world, including the Apa Tani of northeast India. The weaver ties one end of the loom around his or her waist, and fastens the other end to a post. Leaning backward keeps the threads at the correct tension for weaving. Narrow lengths of fabric are woven, and are used to make clothes for the weaver's family.

D
E
S
I
G
N

Communications

THE earliest means of communication were visual. People used hand gestures and signs. These were soon joined by grunts and other simple sounds, which in time became words. Spoken languages developed, using many words and complicated grammar, which gave the languages their structure. As soon as languages were first written down, design became an essential part of communication. Today, movies, television, the Internet, newspapers, books and magazines rely on design to catch the eye, hold the attention, and communicate information quickly and easily. Printed media generally use a combination of words and pictures. A designer makes them attractive by arranging them on the page, choosing different sizes and styles of type, and adding colour backgrounds and borders.

◪ SIMPLE SYMBOLS

Writing first developed in Sumeria (part of present-day Iraq) about 3400 BC, as a way of keeping records of farming, taxes, and trade. It used little pictures, called pictograms, to represent objects. Each pictogram was formed from wedge-shaped marks, made by pressing a reed pen into damp clay.

◪ PICTURE-WRITING

About 3000 BC, the ancient Egyptians invented hieroglyphs – writing that combined pictograms (pictures that portrayed objects) and ideograms (pictures that represented ideas). They were used for recording religious ideas.

◪ PRINTING PRESS

In about 1450, Johannes Gutenberg (c. 1400–68) invented a fast, low-cost method of printing. Metal letters were arranged to form a page of text, then inked and pressed against paper in a printing press like this one from 15th-century Florence.

◼ OVER THE AIR

Radio waves are an invisible form of electromagnetic energy. Italian scientist Guglielmo Marconi (1874–1937) pioneered their use as a means of communication. In 1897, he was the first person to send long-distance messages by radio, over a distance of 19 kilometres. In 1901, Marconi made the first 'wireless' transmission (as early radio was called) across the Atlantic. He was awarded the Nobel Prize for physics in 1909.

◼ THE SHAPE OF THE FUTURE?

The first television broadcasts were made in 1929. Early sets were disguised as pieces of decorative furniture. By 1949, when this 'Predicta' set was made, television was still a rare and expensive luxury, but the design of the 'Predicta' was streamlined and modern, rather than functional and hidden away. Today, there are television sets in most homes in the developed world.

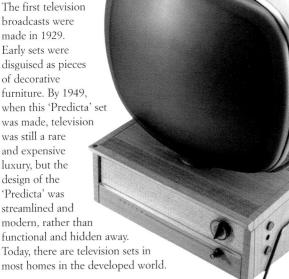

◼ HELLO?

Scottish-born inventor Alexander Graham Bell (1847–1922), who lived and worked in the United States, designed the first telephone in 1876. Telephones introduced a whole new way of communicating, based on a caller speaking to someone they could not see. People had to rely solely on words to convey information, without the help of body language.

TEXT MESSAGES AND EMAILS

In the past, people had to wait days or weeks to receive mail. Today, mobile phones (first widely available in the 1990s) and the Internet allow users to send and receive text messages worldwide in seconds.

Sport

MANY sports and games developed as training for war. Men improved their strength, fitness and battlefield skills by running races, throwing javelins, boxing, wrestling, and shooting arrows. Games played on horseback, such as polo, were used to prepare cavalry fighters for long campaigns. Even games such as chess were useful training for army strategists – and spies! But sports and games were soon played for their own sake. Architects designed stadiums with facilities for players and spectators. During the 20th century, hi-tech designs and modern materials improved equipment such as tennis rackets and speed-bikes, allowing ever-faster speeds to be attained.

◤ OLYMPIC ARCH

Sports grounds, or stadiums, have existed for almost 3000 years. This stone archway marks the entrance to the main race track at Olympia, in Greece. According to tradition, the Olympic Games were first held at Olympia in 776 BC, originally to honour the Greek god Zeus.

◤ FAST, LIGHT AND UNSTEADY

Two-wheeled Roman chariots were fast, light, and easy to manoeuvre. They were originally designed to carry noblemen and army commanders into war, but were soon converted for use in one of Rome's most popular sports – chariot racing. Charioteers drove at breakneck speed around an oval arena, called a hippodrome.

◤ DRESSED TO WIN

During the late 20th century, new 'performance' clothes were designed to help athletes achieve their best. Made from artificial hi-tech fibres, they were tight, soft, light, stretchy, comfortable, and helped draw perspiration away from the skin.

☑ DESIGNED FOR DANGER

Players in some fast-moving sports, such as ice hockey (shown here) or football, run the risk of serious injury if they crash into one another or are hit by hard sticks or balls. For protection, they wear thick, padded clothing, tough boots and gloves, metal helmets and sometimes face masks as well.

THE BEST EQUIPMENT

In a sport like motor racing, the equipment can be as important as the driver's skill. Well-designed cars, like this Porsche built for US 'Indy' races, give their drivers an advantage. Drivers also rely on teams of expert technicians to keep their car in prime condition, or to mend it if it breaks down.

☑ BIG BY DESIGN

Sumo wrestling is an ancient Japanese sport that is still popular today. The men taking part are unusually big and extremely strong. Each wrestler normally weighs more than 160 kilograms, and tries to force his opponent to the ground by holds, trips, pushes and falls, in a series of bouts. The winner gains the most points, awarded by a referee.

▨ 'LITTLE BROTHER OF WAR'

Some Native American peoples played sports to settle quarrels. Instead of fighting, whole villages joined in games like lacrosse – played with a ball and a stick with a net at one end. It was known as 'the little brother of war'.

Travel and transport

FOR most of history, travel was slow, difficult and often dangerous. Only people who had to travel, such as merchants, soldiers and sailors, made frequent long-distance journeys. But over the centuries, engineers have designed ever faster and more efficient vehicles, from the horse and cart to ships, trains, motor cars and aircraft. Since the mid-20th century, the rapid advances in vehicle design have enabled countless people to travel increasingly long distances, both for work and pleasure. Tourism is probably the world's largest industry now, and all over the world, whole resort villages are designed specially for tourists.

◪ SQUARE SAIL

The ancient Egyptians built the earliest-known ships in about 3000 BC. They were made from reeds and, like this slightly later wooden riverboat (c. 2500 BC), they had one square sail. The design of ships' sails did not change until the Middle Ages.

◪ RAILROAD REVOLUTION

The first steam locomotive was designed and built in England by engineer Richard Trevithick, in 1804. It was used to pull carriages along metal tracks. Railways transformed the way people lived. By 1845 (the date of this scene), trains carried factory-made goods to distant markets and food from the country to the fast-growing towns.

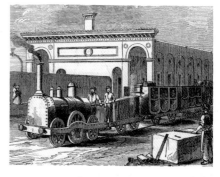

◪ THE FORCE OF THE WIND

The first European ship to have three masts was the caravel of the late 1400s. The next 350 years saw many changes in the design of ships, aimed at increasing their speed. By the 1840s, huge 'clipper' sailing ships like this one were the fastest wind-driven merchant ships ever built. They were able to sail from Asia to Europe, carrying tea and other goods, in less than 100 days.

STIRRUPS

Stirrups are loops with a flat base that are attached to a saddle by straps and support a rider's feet. Until they were invented in China, about AD 500, it was difficult to ride a galloping horse, or to throw a spear from horseback. Stirrups gave riders a strong 'platform' on which to stand.

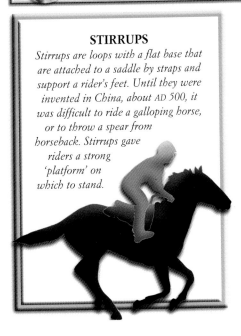

◢ TOP SPEED

The first petrol engine, or internal combustion engine, was designed by German inventors Daimler and Benz in 1885. In 1903, the early Rolls-Royce car (above) held the world record for speed. It could travel for short distances at 134 kilometres per hour. Today, cars provide fast, convenient transportation for millions of people, but they also cause serious environmental pollution.

◢ THE JET AGE

Jet engines, like those on this Boeing 747, work by pushing out a stream of exhaust gases very fast at the rear. This drives the plane forward through the air. The first jet engines were designed in the 1930s by British engineer Frank Whittle. Since the 1960s, fast jet travel has enabled many people to travel abroad for their holidays. Super-fast jet planes are also used by many armed forces for bombing, air attack and reconnaissance.

◢ ANIMAL LOADS

Before the 20th century, people relied on animals to provide power for transport, and to carry heavy loads. Horses, donkeys and mules pulled carriages and carts or were laden with panniers, or baskets, and camels carried heavy loads across deserts. Animal transport was often slow, and could be dangerous. Frightened animals might bolt, throwing off baggage and riders, while sickly animals could die, leaving travellers stranded.

Risk and danger

RISK and danger are part of human life. Some people, like airline test pilots or movie stunt actors, take risks as a way of earning a living. Others have tried to protect themselves from danger by designing and making all kinds of special devices. These range from magic charms and special clothes to protective gadgets built into machines. For some, like emergency aid workers or firefighters, facing risks and dangers is an unpleasant, but necessary, side to helping people in need.

A few people add risks to their 'design for living' by practicing dangerous sports, such as mountain climbing. For them, facing up to death is a way of feeling more alive.

◪ LUCKY CHARM

Many peoples around the world have carried an amulet, or lucky charm to protect them from danger. In ancient Egypt, amulets often showed a scarab, or dung beetle. Scarabs roll a ball of dung over the ground, which reminded the Egyptians of the life-giving Sun rolling across the sky.

◪ DRESSED TO FACE DEATH

In the 16th and 17th centuries, European doctors treating patients with deadly diseases, such as bubonic plague, dressed in unusual protective clothing. They wore long cloaks, leather gloves, close-fitting hats and pointed masks like birds' beaks, stuffed with antiseptic herbs and spices.

WARNING LIGHT

Before modern electronic navigation aids, ships relied on lighthouses to warn them of dangerous rocks. Each lighthouse flashed its own signal pattern, so that sailors could identify their location.

◪ UNDER THE WAVES

Deep-sea divers perform essential tasks in many industries, such as offshore oil and gas drilling, salvaging wrecked ships and their cargoes, and making underwater surveys to help geologists. They also work for the police and coast guards, helping in rescue operations. This submersible ship is designed to carry divers safely from support ships on the surface to their work on the seabed.

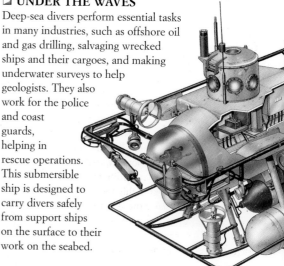

▣ DANGEROUS WORK

For movie stunt actors, taking risks is a way of earning a living. All kinds of devices have been designed to make their acts look more dangerous than they really are. A jump or fall from a building, for example, may be less far than it appears on camera, and will be cushioned by an air mattress.

▣ OUT OF THIS WORLD

Astronauts face all kinds of risks in space. Inside their spaceships, they breathe a special mixture of gases. Outside, working in space, they have to wear heavy protective suits, which provide them with oxygen to breathe, supply heat to stop them freezing to death and protect their bodies from harmful radiation.

▢ FIRE!

Firefighters are trained to face danger in order to help save others in emergencies. They rely on special clothing, like this fireproof suit, to survive in extreme conditions. Made from the latest highly resistant materials, it insulates the skin from excessive heat. The multi-layered face-mask is also designed to prevent hot ash from entering the firefighter's mouth and nose.

DESIGN

Weapons and warfare

WEAPONS are designed to kill or to inflict serious injuries. Over the centuries, engineers have designed fearsome machines for attack or defence in war. Some were adaptations of inventions first designed for peaceful purposes. Barbed wire, for example, was originally designed as a fence for cattle, but during World War I (1914–18) it was used to entangle thousands of soldiers on the battlefields of Europe. Other wartime inventions were later modified for peaceful functions. Gunpowder, invented in China as a weapon in about AD 1000, was soon used in small amounts to create fireworks, which have delighted people at special celebrations ever since.

▨ EXPLOSIVE!

Gunpowder was first used in Europe from about AD 1300. Early cannons fired heavy stone or metal balls at defensive walls. At first they were hardly more effective than weapons that catapulted rocks, but gradually their range improved and they could be placed farther back from the enemy.

⬑ SIEGE ENGINES

In medieval Europe (c. AD 1000–1500), huge 'siege engines' were used to attack the defensive stone walls of castles and cities. Some were designed to smash holes in stonework, or to hurl rocks over the walls. Others were shaped like tall, movable towers. They carried soldiers close to the castle, to give them a better chance of climbing inside.

◨ MACHINE GUNS

The first machine guns were
invented in 1862 by
American inventors
Richard Gatling
and Wilson Agar.
They were designed to
fire a continuous stream of
bullets much more quickly
than any hand-held gun.
Machine guns were
expensive, but gave any army
who owned them a great
advantage over their enemies.

TRENCHES

*During World War I
(1914–18), millions of
men fought in the
trenches of Belgium and
France. Trenches were
deep slits dug into the
ground. Although
designed as places to hide
from enemy fire, they
became death wtraps.*

◨ INVISIBLE?

During the late 20th century, new
aircraft like this B2 'stealth' bomber were
designed to be invisible to radar- or heat-
detecting devices. Able to fly unobserved over
enemy territory, they can carry out precision
attacks on targets using laser-guided bombs.
But the unusual design
of 'stealth' aircraft makes
them both difficult to
fly and expensive to
operate and maintain.

◨ FLYING BOMBS

Missiles are powerful 'flying bombs', first used in
1942. Modern missiles are designed to
destroy a wide range of targets. They can
be fitted with radar or infrared
equipment to steer themselves,
or can be guided by human
operators. Some carry
nuclear warheads.

◧ UNSTOPPABLE

Tanks were first used in
battle in France in 1917.
The 'caterpillar' tracks
that carry them along are
designed to cope with
the most difficult terrain,
and can flatten obstacles
that would stop wheeled
vehicles in their tracks.
Armour plating protects
the soldiers inside.

Worship

SOME of the world's most beautiful buildings, finest works of art and greatest treasures were designed for use in worship. Rich patrons provided the money to pay for religious objects, while artists and architects lavished time, skill and the best materials on creations designed for religious use. Why did they do this at a time when many people around them were desperately poor? Partly, they wanted to provide a splendid home for their god or gods. To show that a holy site was special, religious leaders made sure that it was clean, beautiful, richly decorated, and kept in good repair. Sometimes patrons and artists wanted to create a memorial to themselves, or to leave a lasting monument for others to admire.

◩ MAGICAL ART

In ancient Egypt, art was believed to have a magic power that could keep a person's spirit alive. This tomb painting is of the Sun god Re (or Ra), the mythical first king of Egypt.

◩ PLACE OF BLESSINGS

For Hindus, a temple, or *mandir*, is a very special place. It is designed to house a *murti* – a holy statue of a goddess or god. Visitors to the temple bring sweets, fruit or flowers to offer to the god, and are blessed by temple priests in return. This Hindu temple is on the island of Bali, Indonesia.

◪ SKILFULLY CRAFTED FROM MUD

The magnificent mosque in Djenne, in central Mali, north Africa, is the largest mud-brick building in the world. Built in 1906, its design was based on that of the great 13th-century mosque that stood on the site for about 600 years. Every year after the rainy season, the smooth layer of mud that covers the bricks has to be repaired.

◄ HOLY HOMES

The ancient town of Çatal Hüyük, in Turkey, dates from about 6000 BC. Evidence suggests that many of the houses were built as shrines – they had ox skulls fixed to the walls, and many bodies were found buried under the floors. No one knows who was worshipped there, but it may have been a mother-goddess.

◣ DIVINE DECORATIONS

Distinctive onion-shaped domes decorate Orthodox churches all over Russia, including St. Basil's Cathedral in Moscow. The Orthodox Church is one of the four main divisions of Christianity. It parted from the other three soon after AD 1000. Orthodox churches contain icons – holy portraits of Jesus, the Virgin Mary, and Christian saints.

◄ GOD IS HERE

To Jewish people, lighted candles burning in a *menorah* – a multi-branched candlestick – are a sign of God's presence. Traditionally, a great golden *menorah* was kept constantly burning in the ancient Jewish temple in Jerusalem. Today, many Jewish people light candles at the yearly festival of Hanukkah, and on other special days.

PILGRIMS

In the past, many Christians travelled long distances to places where saints' remains were displayed in specially designed caskets called reliquaries. The pilgrims believed that seeing, or touching, the remains would bring blessings, and might even cure illness.

Performing Arts

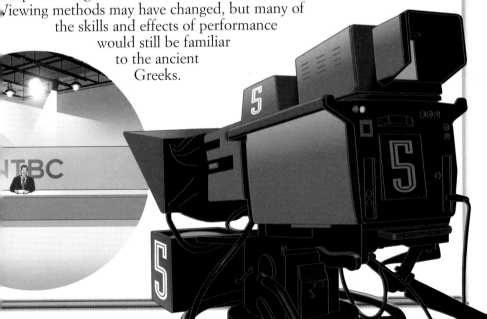

IN ANCIENT Greece, some 18,000 people would pack the seats of giant outdoor theatres to watch actors play out scenes of great tragedies. The excitement of watching performers presenting a story, ballet, or stand-up comedy is just as strong today. But performances no longer have to be presented to live audiences: film preserves them forever, and allows elaborate possibilities through locations, camera angles, and special effects. Through television we have the performing arts beamed into our own homes. Viewing methods may have changed, but many of the skills and effects of performance would still be familiar to the ancient Greeks.

P
E
R
F
O
R
M
I
N
G

A
R
T
S

Performer and audience

WE are all performers. We perform when we tell a joke or recount a story. Performing is part of human nature. But people who make a living by performing have to be especially good at it. They have to be able to hold the attention of an audience, and entertain them; otherwise – quite simply – they will not be paid to perform again. Performing is an ancient craft. Professional entertainers have been making a living by performing since ancient times – earning gifts of money, or perhaps just a meal, at markets, at the courts of kings and nobles, or in specially built theatres. And there have always been storytellers, actors, conjurers, comedians, acrobats, and dancers – just as there are today.

◪ JUGGLERS OF OLD
Tomb paintings from the Etruscan civilization in Italy, dating from more than 2500 years ago, show a man and a woman juggling. The basic skills of juggling, and the trick of keeping as many objects in the air at the same time, remain the same today.

◪ ELABORATE THEATRES
The earliest theatres, built by the ancient Greeks, were open to the skies. But over time covered theatres developed, and became more elaborate. The King's Theatre, built in 1790, was the largest in London, and one of the grandest. Boxes overlooking the stage gave small parties privacy.

◪ ESCAPOLOGIST
The Hungarian-born American Harry Houdini (1874–1926) was one of the world's greatest showmen, and the most famous 'escapologist', or escape artist, of all time. Using clever tricks, he was able to escape from chains and handcuffs while locked in a safe or immersed in a tank of water.

PANTOMIME

Pantomimes such as Dick Whittington *are full of knock about fun. Audiences are often encouraged to participate by shouting out warnings to the 'good' characters. The pantomime tradition developed from the Italian comic plays of the 1500s called* Commedia dell'Arte.

■ PROFESSIONAL STORYTELLERS

One of the simplest, oldest and most effective forms of entertainment is storytelling – an ancient art that has been almost killed off by television. Professional storytellers earned a living by recounting great tales of adventure, love, myth and heroism. A good storyteller can paint vivid pictures in words, enabling listeners to see characters and scenes in their imaginations.

◨ ENTERTAINING JESTERS

In medieval times, kings and nobles often employed jesters – professional clowns – to provide entertainment by joking and making fun of daily events. Dressed in 'motley' (shown here), the jester was a 'fool' whom no one took seriously. Because of this, he was able to speak the truth when no one else dared.

■ VENICE CARNIVAL

The annual Carnival in Venice, Italy, was the most wild and extravagant fancy dress party in Europe during the 1700s, but the French emperor Napoleon put a stop to it when he invaded Italy in 1797. In 1979 the tradition was revived. Hundreds of people dress up in beautiful masks and costumes like these.

The circus

THE circus is one of the oldest forms of popular entertainment. The word 'circus' comes from the ancient Greek word for a ring. The round performing area inside a modern circus tent is called an arena, from the Latin for sand. In Roman times, circus arenas were built for chariot races, gladiator fights and other popular spectacles. During the 18th century a new kind of circus developed, in which trained horses and other animals were made to perform in the acts. They were soon joined by acrobats and clowns. The shows were originally held indoors, but before long the troupe took to the road, taking their own theatre – a tent, or big top' – with them. Circuses still follow this tradition. Today's circus acts appear ever more daring, but are actually safer.

◪ COMICAL CLOWNS

No circus is complete without clowns, the comedians of the show. Their comical outfits and face paint make it immediately clear that they are not going to do anything remotely serious, scary or even successful. Their humour is almost entirely visual, based on actions, not words. Slap-stick humour – throwing foam cakes or custard pies in someone's face, for example – plays a key part in their acts.

◪ ACROBATS

Acrobats, such as these Chinese circus performers, develop their extraordinary skills of balancing, bending, jumping and tumbling through years of practice. They need strong muscles, very flexible bodies, supreme control and great courage.

◪ GIANT CIRCUS TENT

Canada's world-famous Cirque du Soleil, founded in 1984, performs in a traditional striped 'big top'. These giant circus tents are specially designed to be packed up easily for moving to another location. Some are vast: in 1924, 16,700 people packed into a big top to see the Ringling Brothers and Barnum & Bailey Circus, Kansas.

◩ FLYING CIRCUS

A very different kind of circus takes place in the air. Small airplanes can perform stunning aerial acrobatics, looping the loop, going into free falls, and weaving around other airplanes at breathtaking speed. Sometimes 'wing walkers' demonstrate their courage by standing on the wing of the plane, strapped to a support.

◩ TRADITIONAL CIRCUS

In 1768, Englishman Philip Astley launched a show that included horse-riding acts and acrobats. This kind of traditional circus lasted for some 200 years. Today, animal acts are less popular, and many circuses now have no animals.

HIGH WIRE ACTS

Daring high wire acts aim to make the audience fear for the safety of the performer, or tightrope walker (originally rope was used). With a superb sense of balance, the performer walks high above the ground along a steel cable, which is held taut to give support. Often a safety net is used.

◩ THE FLYING TRAPEZE

The flying trapeze act was invented in 1859 by the French acrobat Jules Léotard (who gave his name to the gym and dance outfit called a leotard). Performers leap and dive between swings suspended high above the ground. When performing as part of a team, one trapeze artist dangling from a swing will catch another by the hands as the acrobat somersaults through the air.

The origins of drama

STAGE plays, or drama, originated in ancient Greece, where religious festivals of singing, dancing and acting were held to honour the god Dionysus. Over time, plays written for these festivals became more elaborate. There were two kinds. Tragedies told agonizing, emotionally-charged stories about nobles, heroes and gods. Comedies were usually about ordinary people in funny situations. These same categories have survived to this day. Greek and Roman theatres were open to the skies, but later, plays were performed in any indoor space. The first purpose-built theatre with a stage was built in Italy in 1618.

◪ GREEK ACTORS

In ancient Greece, all the actors wore masks. Different kinds of mask represented a certain kind of character. By changing the mask, an actor could play a number of different roles in the same play. All Greek actors were men.

◪ COMMEDIA DELL'ARTE

Italian comic plays known as *Commedia dell'Arte* began in the 1500s. Playing a set of familiar characters – the pretty girl Columbine, her rich old father Pantaloon, Harlequin, and Punch the clown – travelling players entertained the crowds with dance, songs and slapstick comedy.

◪ MARCEL MARCEAU

Mime is a specialized kind of acting performed entirely without words. Mime artists use movements and gestures to indicate an imaginary world around them. The world's best-known mime artist is Frenchman Marcel Marceau (b. 1923).

KABUKI THEATRE

The type of traditional Japanese play called Kabuki developed in the 1700s. It combines richly costumed theatre, poetry, singing, music and dance. No women take part, so men perform the women's roles.

MYSTERY PLAY

In medieval times, worker's guilds presented open-air plays based on stories from the Bible. They were called 'mystery plays' but the term really comes from the Latin *ministerium*, a guild or occupation. At religious festivals, different guilds played out episodes from the Bible, from the Creation to Christ's crucifixion.

INDIAN THEATRE

The southern Indian tradition of theatre called *kathakali* was originally performed in temple ceremonies, and perhaps dates back 2000 years. The actors, wearing dramatic make-up and rich costumes, tell stories from Hindu mythology, through elaborate dance-like gestures and facial expressions. Training begins at the age of five and lasts for 20 years.

EXAGGERATED STYLE

The greatest British actor in the late 1800s was Henry Irving (1838–1905), here pictured playing the lead role in Shakespeare's *Hamlet*. In the big and busy theatres of Irving's day, actors had to make grand gestures and speak in firm, loud voices – a style that today would be thought 'melodramatic', or exaggerated.

Modern theatre

UNTIL the late 19th century, most plays were about extraordinary events set in the past, or comedies that poked fun at the way people live. Then a new set of writers began to make dramas about the modern world using situations that the audiences themselves might recognize from their own lives – popularly called 'kitchen sink' dramas. Since then, plays have become even more varied. Today they range from realistic plays that portray a 'slice of life' to stylized, anti-realistic fantasies that make no attempt to represent real life at all.

◪ STANISLAVSKY

The Russian actor and director Constantin Stanislavsky (1863–1938) revolutionized modern acting. He encouraged actors to work out what their characters would think and feel in the play. This approach is known as 'Method Acting'.

◪ IBSEN

The Norwegian playwright Henrik Ibsen (1828–1906) is known as the 'Founder of Modern Drama'. He was the first major dramatist to write about modern people and the social issues of the day. This scene is from his play *Enemy of the People.*

◪ LOOK BACK IN ANGER

When the play *Look Back in Anger* by the British writer John Osborne (1929–94) was first performed in 1956, it caused an outrage. It deals with the conflicts of an ill-matched couple leading an ordinary life. Osborne became known as one of a group of writers called the 'Angry Young Men'. This scene is from the film of 1959.

POLITICAL THEATRE

Some modern plays aim to make a political point. In Soviet Russia, actors were employed by the government to put on plays that taught lessons about the benefits of the Soviet system.

◼ A DIFFERENT VIEWPOINT

The British dramatist Tom Stoppard (b. 1937) first came to notice with his play *Rosencrantz and Guildenstern are Dead* (1966). In this farce, or exaggerated comedy, Stoppard takes a sideways look at Shakespeare's tragedy *Hamlet* by basing his play on two of Shakespeare's characters. Through his clever and often very witty writing, he is also able to touch upon serious issues.

◻ SHOCKHEADED PETER

The stage play *Shockheaded Peter* (1998) is a theatrical version of the old German illustrated children's book *Struwelpeter*, which makes vicious fun of old moral tales. The play uses music, puppets, bizarre scenery and exaggerated performances to recreate the weird world of the original book.

◼ MODERN-DRESS SHAKESPEARE

Old plays can be given a new twist by re-staging them in a new era. The plays of William Shakespeare (1564–1616) are often re-worked in this way, such as this 1996 version of *A Midsummer Night's Dream*. The effect is to give new meaning to the words. The language is still that of Shakespeare, but a modern setting can show how it is still relevant in the modern world.

Casting to curtain call

GOOD theatre needs good performers. A weak play can be made excellent by good actors, and a good play can be ruined by poor or unconvincing acting. Good acting comes from a mixture of natural skill, practice and experience. But a theatrical performance is really teamwork – from the moment someone has the idea of putting on a play to the final curtain call, when the actors bow at the end of the performance. One of the most important members of the team never appears on stage at all: the director. He or she is responsible for the look of the play and way it is performed.

THE ROLE OF THE DIRECTOR

Once the director has chosen the actors for the play, rehearsals can begin. At rehearsals, the director guides the actors in how to say their lines and move around the stage. The director also makes decisions about what kind of scenery to use, the style of costumes and the lighting, and coordinates all the people involved. Here the director is rehearsing a scene from the opera
La Bohème.

FINDING THE ACTORS

One of the first tasks in putting on a play is choosing the right actors for the various parts. Actors are invited to an audition by the director, who asks them to read from the script or to perform a short piece on stage. The job of deciding which actor is best suited for each part is called 'casting'.

■ THE ROLE OF THE PROMPT

Almost all actors become nervous before they go on stage, and once in front of an audience they sometimes forget their lines. It is the job of the 'prompt' who remains hidden at the side of the stage, to follow the script throughout a performance, and help an actor who 'dries up' on stage by whispering the next line. Even the best actors – such as Laurence Olivier and Vivien Leigh, seen here in *Romeo and Juliet* – have needed prompting.

SCRIPT

The very first stage of making a play, usually, is writing the script. A script generally consists of two elements – the speeches and dialogue spoken by the characters, and stage directions, which tell the actors where and when to move.

■ PRACTISE MAKES PERFECT

Actors attend many rehearsals before a play or film is shown to the public. At rehearsals, the actors and the director work at coordinating words and movements, as well as exits and entrances. The actors give each other 'cues' or signals, so that they know when to speak or do something. Here Barbra Streisand is rehearsing a dance in *Funny Girl* (1968).

■ TEAM WORK

Many stage shows require teamwork from the cast, particularly if the show includes extravagant musical routines, as in *The Boyfriend* (film version 1971). A special director of dance, called a choreographer, teaches the actors the dance routines. They must work together as a team until they can make it all look smooth and easy!

Inside a theatre

PUTTING on a play involves many more people than just the director and the actors. There are set designers and set builders, lighting technicians, costume designers and wardrobe assistants, make-up artists and stage managers and stage hands who organize the scene-changes. Any theatre also has 'front-of-house' staff, who sell and check the tickets and look after the audience. While the actors come and go, many of the people working backstage and front-of-house are employed permanently by the theatre. A theatre manager must ensure that a production can cover all its costs, and even make a profit.

◪ SCENERY DESIGN

A play's scenery provides the background setting. Usually painted onto flat screens, it may represent a garden, the inside of a house, or whatever is appropriate. The design may be sumptuous or very sparse, depending on what effect the director wants to create. It must also provide places for the actors to make their entrances and exits.

PROPS

Any moveable object on the stage – such as a gun in a drawer or a letter on a desk – is known as a 'prop' (short for 'property'). It is the job of the stagehands to make sure that the props are in the right place on stage for the actors to use.

◪ THEATRE INTERIOR

A big theatre is a highly complex building. The audience sees only a small part of it as they enter through the foyer and find their seat in the auditorium. Behind the stage, which is in the middle of the building, are large areas used for storing scenery, wardrobe rooms for storing costumes, dressing and make-up rooms, rehearsal areas and a canteen for the actors and stage crew.

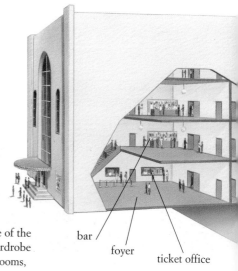

bar

foyer

ticket office

◨ THE EFFECTS OF LIGHTING

While a play is still in rehearsal, lighting technicians work with the director to plan the lighting for the play very carefully. Different scenes require different effects, from moonlit woodland shadows to a bright interior, a spotlit star or a sudden flash of lightning. During a performance, most lights are operated from a lighting console, which allows the lighting technician to switch the lights on and off, or change or fade them 'on cue', exactly when needed.

◧ COSTUME AND MAKE-UP

Actors can be transformed into their characters by their costumes and make-up. Costume designers help to turn the director's vision of how the characters should look into reality. The costumes are either specially made or bought. Make-up artists can also completely change an actor's appearance. The make-up is often applied boldly, because it has to be seen at a great distance and under the glare of the stage lights.

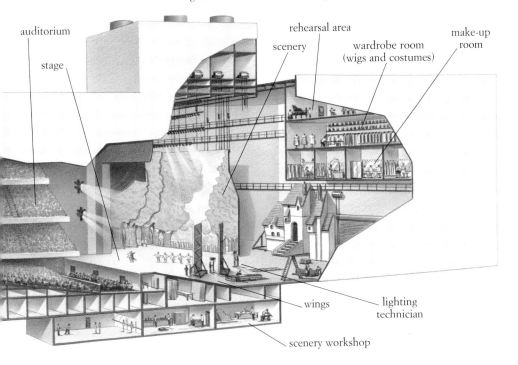

auditorium

stage

rehearsal area

scenery

wardrobe room
(wigs and costumes)

make-up
room

wings

lighting
technician

scenery workshop

Opera and musicals

AN OPERA is a kind of sung drama. The first operas were created in Venice in about 1600. Early operas often related tales from classical mythology, but later works ranged from tales of love and comic misunderstandings, to great tragedies involving trickery, murder, sickness and war. Of course, in real life people do not go around singing to each other! But opera allows the performers not simply to sing what they want to say, but also to express their innermost thoughts. Musicals offer a more popular and approachable blend of singing and acting, often appealing to a wider audience.

◪ BAYREUTH

The German composer Richard Wagner (1813–83) wrote some of the most magnificent and ambitious operas, most based on German myths. He built a theatre to mount these huge productions in his home town of Bayreuth, in Bavaria, and founded the annual festival of his work.

◪ MADAME BUTTERFLY

One of Italy's greatest opera composers Giacomo Puccini (1858–1924) wrote *Madame Butterfly* in 1904, at a time when there was a great interest in Japanese culture in Europe. It tells of a tragic marriage between a Japanese woman and an American naval officer, Lieutenant Pinkerton, and ends in her suicide.

◪ THE MARRIAGE OF FIGARO

Wolfgang Amadeus Mozart (1756–91) wrote this delightful, funny opera in about 1786. Based on a French play of the same name, it relates the complicated love story of a count who tries to steal the girlfriend of his servant, Figaro. Some of the songs are deeply moving.

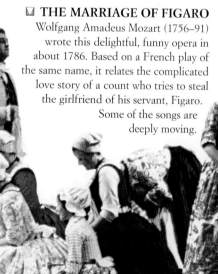

OKLAHOMA!

The successful partnership between Richard Rodgers (1902–79), who wrote music, and Oscar Hammerstein II (1895–1960), who wrote words, produced some of the best-known American musicals, including *Oklahoma!*, *The King and I*, *South Pacific,* and *The Sound of Music*. Their skill was in combining popular songs with a good story.

PLACIDO DOMINGO

Opera has produced some great stars, who are celebrated for the quality of their voices. They command huge fees to sing at opera houses around the world. One such star is the Spanish tenor Placido Domingo (b. 1941), here seen in a 1983 film version of *La Traviata*, by the great Italian opera composer, Giuseppe Verdi (1813–1901).

ARIAS

Many of the most famous operas contain 'songs' sung by one of the lead singers. These are known as arias, *the Italian word for an 'air' or 'tune'. A famous example is the hugely popular 'Nessun Dorma',* ♩♪♩ *from Puccini's opera* Turandot.

LES MISÉRABLES

Early musicals were generally lighthearted, but the huge success of *Les Misérables* (1980), with music by French composer Claude-Michel Schönberg and words by Alain Boublil and Herbert Kretzmer, showed that more serious subjects were possible. Based on the novel by Victor Hugo, it is set during the French Revolution.

The world of dance

DANCE is one of the oldest of all the performing arts. Traditional dancing has formed part of almost all cultures around the world. No doubt originally it was an activity to participate in, rather than to watch. But early on, dancers developed performances designed to be watched by an audience. While folk dances remain firmly rooted in tradition, new forms of dancing are developing all the time, in response to the kinds of music people like to listen to, and the ways they choose to entertain themselves.

◪ AFRICAN DANCE

Dance in Africa is usually performed to the beat of drums. Many traditional dances were performed for special occasions such as marriages, harvest or war. They are often highly energetic.

◪ GREEK TRADITION

Greece has one of the most lively traditions of folk dancing in the modern world. Traditional dancing is still widely performed, especially at weddings. While the traditions of the old folk dances are carefully respected and preserved, Greek dance is constantly changing. The *syrtaki,* for instance, is a new dance, introduced in 1964 through the film *Zorba the Greek.*

◪ ABORIGINAL RITUALS

For the Aborigines of Australia, dance formed a part of religious rituals and ceremonies. There were once more than 500 different Aboriginal tribes, and each had its own distinctive style of dance. Most involved imitations of animals or spirits, and were accompanied by chanting.

WHIRLING DERVISHES

Sufis form a mystical group within Islam, and are found in parts of the Middle East and North Africa. In one of their rituals, they chant the name of God to rhythmic music and clapping, and begin to swirl around in a trancelike state. These dancers are sometimes called 'whirling dervishes'.

GRACEFUL MOVEMENTS

The traditional dances of the Indonesian island of Bali were mostly all devised for performance at Hindu temple ceremonies. Dancers begin their rigorous training at a very young age – girl dancers are considered to be at their peak aged about 12. The graceful, complex movements are danced to the music of gamelan orchestras.

BREAK DANCING

An acrobatic style of dance developed in New York during the 1980s, as an accompaniment to the new kind of music called rap and hip-hop culture. It involved much more energetic movements than previous dance styles, and greater use of the hands and body on the floor, with spinning and gymnastic floor movements. Tracksuit bottoms and running shoes were part of the standard dress.

BALLROOM DANCING

In the past in Europe, dances and balls gave young men and women a rare opportunity to meet. They learned formal dances, such as the waltz or the polka. The tango (shown here) is a racier type of dance that developed in Argentina in the early 1900s.

The ballet story

BALLET originated in Italy and France about 300 years ago as stage performances that told a story through movements to music. 'Classical ballet' developed into a disciplined style of dancing that required supreme control of the body and dancing on the tips of the toes. All the movements are planned and rehearsed in great detail. A new approach to ballet developed during the 20th century, in which some of the disciplines of classical ballet were dropped to permit more freedom of movement. Good ballet brings together technically superb performance with a convincing artistic interpretation of the music. It produces a mixture of sight and sound that is deeply satisfying to watch, but may be hard to express in words.

◢ ISADORA DUNCAN

Isadora Duncan (1878–1927) developed a style of dancing based on Greek classical dance. Performing barefoot in flowing robes, she introduced free expression, and was highly influential in the development of modern dance.

◁ LA SYLPHIDE

Classical ballet became an international success with *La Sylphide* (1832). It was the work of a bold new generation of dancers, and it demonstrated the charm and artistic beauty of this highly disciplined form of dancing. In the ballet, a Scottish peasant forsakes his bride-to-be for the love of a winged sprite, who represents a happiness he can never attain.

▭ THE RED SHOES

The British film *The Red Shoes* (1948) starring Moira Shearer, tells the story of a young dancer who becomes impassioned by her art, and is saved from obsession by a young composer. Its beautifully filmed dance sequences had a major impact on the British public's appreciation of ballet.

☑ POSITIONS AND POINTS

In classical ballet, all movements end with one of the five positions. These were devised in the 1700s primarily as a way of making the feet look elegant. Classical ballerinas also dance on the tips of their toes, or 'points'. Their shoes are stiffened to help them.

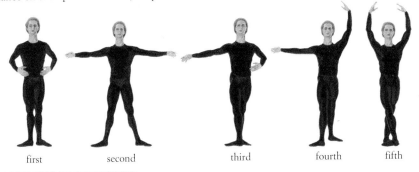

first   second   third   fourth   fifth

BALLETS RUSSES

The Ballets Russes was launched in 1909 by manager Sergei Diaghilev. The mix of modern dance and music often shocked audiences, and even caused a riot in the theatre.

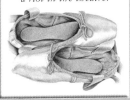

☐ CELEBRATED DANCER

The Russian Vaslav Nijinsky (1890–1950) was one of the most celebrated ballet dancers of all time. He became famous for his dancing with the Ballets Russes. Roles included *L'Après-midi d'un faune* ('A faun's afternoon') in 1912. His career was cut short when he became mentally unwell in 1919.

☑ BOLSHOI BALLET

The famous Bolshoi Ballet was founded in Moscow as a dance school in 1773. The Bolshoi Theatre was built in 1856. The ballet school is famous for the athletic skills of its dancers, and its large-scale performances – this one is of the 1907 ballet *Les Sylphides*, originally choreographed by Mikhail Fokine (1880–1942).

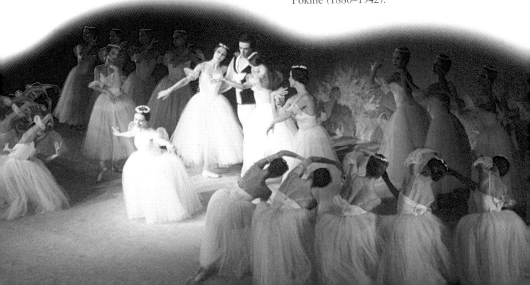

Powerful puppets

IN INDONESIA it is still possible to watch huge battle scenes from the great epics of Hindu mythology performed by just one man using an oil lamp, a white screen and a box full of flat, cut-out puppets on sticks. By contrast, an audience might be moved to tears by a love story performed by two socks on a pair of hands. Puppets can cast this extraordinary range of illusions, and are capable of creating far bigger and stranger stage effects than human actors. They can create theatre on a miniature scale and on a grand scale. There are three main kinds of puppets: shadow puppets, glove puppets and string puppets, or marionettes.

◪ VENTRILOQUISTS

Ventriloquism is the art of speaking without moving the lips, and making the sound appear to come from a puppet, or 'dummy'. The audience is led to believe that the dummy is having a conversation, or an argument, with the ventriloquist, to comic effect. Here the ventriloquist is American Edgar Bergen (1903–1978).

◪ INDONESIAN SHADOW PUPPETS

Traditional Indonesian shadow puppets are cut from leather. A stick supports the back and provides a handle for the *dalang* (puppeteer) to hold at the base, while two thin sticks are used to operate the hands. The *dalang* sits behind the screen onto which the shadows are projected, and the audience sits in front of it.

◪ PUNCH AND JUDY

This traditional English form of puppet show, based on the old Italian farces of the *Commedia dell'Arte*, dates back to the 1700s. The stories revolve around the cruel and boastful Mr. Punch and his loud-mouthed wife Judy. Although performed for children, at parties or at the beach, the comic story involves the death of a baby, wife-beating, murder and imprisonment.

◪ MARIONETTES

String puppets, or marionettes, like this one from Thailand, hang on strings from an X-shaped pair of bars. The puppeteer holds the bars with one hand, allowing the puppet to dangle onto a small stage. The other hand operates the strings, which are usually attached to the hands, knees, feet, and back.

◪ ANIMATRONICS

In recent decades puppets have become much more complex. 'Animatronics' – remote-control electronics assisted by computers – are used to animate, or bring alive, a puppet (often an animal). The puppet builders and operators can move many tiny parts of the puppet, such as its facial features. Famous animatronic film creatures include the gremlins.

PINOCCHIO

The famous Italian tale about a naughty puppet called Pinocchio was first written in 1883 by the author known as Collodi. The puppet, made from a magical piece of wood, laughs and cries like a child. Pinocchio soon shows his maker that he has a life of his own, and goes off on all kinds of strange adventures.

◪ THE MUPPETS

The world's most popular puppets of recent years are the Muppets, created by America's Jim Henson (1936–90). They are essentially glove puppets with rods attached to the arms. Kermit the Frog, the first character, was invented in 1955, followed by many others, including blonde Miss Piggy. The Muppet Show (1976–81) was watched by 235 million people worldwide.

Origins of motion picture

WHEN the French brothers Auguste and Louis Lumière made the first-ever movie in 1895, they had no idea that they were laying the foundations of one of the great modern art forms. But it soon became clear that cinema could offer an inexpensive and exciting alternative to theatre. The early movies (mostly comedies) were 'silent' and so could be enjoyed by audiences around the world, regardless of language. Soon, however, directors realized that film was not simply a way to create mass entertainment – it could also be a means of serious artistic expression.

◪ EADWEARD MUYBRIDGE

Early photographers looked for a way to take photos that gave the impression of movement. In the 1880s, Eadweard Muybridge (1830–1904) set up groups of cameras with threads attached to the shutters, so movement could be recorded in quick succession. After printing the photographs, he ran them together in his 'zoepraxiscope' which gave the impression of motion, similar to this early French film.

◪ CINÉMATOGRAPHE

Photographers knew that they could create the illusion of motion by making and showing numerous pictures one after the other. But they did not have the means to do this until the Lumière brothers invented the 'cinématographe,' a device that combined the camera and the projector.

◪ CHARLIE CHAPLIN

Movies were silent until 1927. Instead of speaking, the actors told the story through mime. The occasional sentence of text would also appear on a black screen, giving the audience a hint about the plot. Comedy was one of the most popular forms of the silent cinema, and the greatest star was the English actor Charlie Chaplin (1889–1977). He acted the part of the 'little tramp' in numerous movies, such as *The Kid* (1921), and could be hilarious, idiotic, cunning and pathetic.

EARLY PROJECTORS

One of the great breakthroughs of motion pictures was projecting pictures onto a screen, imitating a theatre. In fact, projectors had been invented for motion picture shows, even before the invention of film.

◻ GREAT WESTERN TRAIN ROBBERY

One of the very first types of American motion picture was the Western. *The Great Train Robbery* was made in 1903, just eight years after motion pictures were invented. At this time, no film lasted much longer than 10 minutes. They were shown to the public in travelling shows and makeshift halls.

◻ CELLULOID

The key to the development of films was celluloid – a continuous strip of flexible plastic film that was stored on reels, like this one of 1931. Celluloid was first used to make motion pictures in 1889. First, a quick succession of photographs was taken using the film. Then light was projected through the developed film onto the screen. Before celluloid, it was not possible to run pictures one after the other so effectively.

◻ SILENT STAR

One of the greatest stars of the silent movie era was the Italian-American Rudolph Valentino (1895–1926). He played romantic leads in films such as *The Sheikh* (1921), and was nicknamed 'the Great Lover'. When he died suddenly aged just 31, some 80,000 emotional mourners paid their respects as his body lay in state in New York.

Colour and special effects

EARLY film makers knew that they could only really compete with theatre if they added sound to their films. This was achieved in 1927, when the *The Jazz Singer*, starring Al Jolson, was released – it was the first 'talkie'. In fact, not everyone welcomed sound. Some of the stars of the silent movies lost their jobs because they had unsuitable voices. And audiences had to learn to be quiet to listen to the film. Another major development was the introduction of colour a few years later. Recently, the use of computer-generated images for special effects has had great impact on film making.

◩ FIRST COLOUR MOVIE
Early film makers made hand-coloured movies as early as 1896. But the first movie in Three-Color Technicolor film was *Becky Sharp* (1935), starring Miriam Hopkins.

◪ BATTLESHIP POTEMKIN
Some early film makers realized that they could create powerful effects using a technique called 'montage' – putting together different shots so that they cut from one to the next in quick succession. This was very effectively done in the Russian film *Battleship Potemkin* (1925).

◪ SPACESHIPS
Models and computer technology are used to create some stunning visual effects, such as the huge spaceship in *Independence Day* (1996). Developments in this field have been rapid since the success of films such as *2001: A Space Odyssey* (1968) and the *Star Wars* trilogy (from 1977). Now, if the effects are not entirely convincing, audiences do not bother to see the movie.

◩ CLOSE-UP SHOTS
Film makers soon realized that film had certain advantages over theatre. A close-up shot, for example, allows the actor to convey subtle changes of emotions. This close-up is of actress Michelle Pfeiffer.

◳ STUNT ACTION

A leading actor
cannot risk getting hurt
in an action scene. So the
director uses a specialist stunt actor
to take the star's place. The stunt
actor is trained to crash cars, jump from
moving trains, or leap through fire –
and do it safely, as in this scene from
the action film *Blown Away* (1994).

◳ SINKING SHIP

For the famous Hollywood blockbuster *Titanic*
(1997), starring Leonardo di Caprio and Kate
Winslet, computer-generated animation was used
for many of the outside shots of the ship. But for the
scenes of the sinking, the stars had to perform in
thousands of gallons of real water!

LOUIS B. MAYER
*One of the great early
Hollywood producers was the
Russian-born American Louis B.
Mayer (1885–1957). He
founded Metro-Goldwyn-Mayer
(MGM) in 1924.*

Making movies

IT IS SAID that film is the most complete of all the art forms, because it combines acting, visual images, music, and often dance. All these elements have to be carefully brought together on strips of celluloid – a process that requires a great deal of organization and large sums of money. A film usually starts as a film script. The director has to be able to visualize the written words so that he or she can turn them into images on screen. Filming is only part of the process. Once complete, the film has to be edited and combined with a soundtrack of voices, music and noises that go with any special effects.

◣ STORYBOARD

A director may plan a film using a 'storyboard' – a sequence of sketches that show roughly how each scene will look. This visual record also helps to ensure that small details remain constant throughout the filming.

◲ LEARNING THE SCRIPT

Film actors learn their words from a script, just as stage actors do. But in film making, the scenes are often shot in the wrong order and are edited into the right order later. So actors – like Marilyn Monroe, seen here in *Gentlemen Prefer Blondes* (1953) – learn their parts scene-by-scene.

◪ THE POWER OF LIGHTING

Lighting plays a major part in the 'look' of a film, whether it is shot outdoors on location, or indoors on a studio set. Backlighting is used here to dramatic effect in a scene from *A Clockwork Orange* (1971), by director Stanley Kubrick (1928–99).

HOLLYWOOD

◪ THE HOME OF FILM

In 1911, pioneer film makers went to a remote settlement called Hollywood, near Los Angeles, to film Westerns, because it had a suitably dry, scrubby landscape. Within two years it had become the centre of American film making and it has dominated the industry worldwide ever since.

◪ THE DIRECTOR

A director's task is to oversee every aspect of the way a movie is made – from scriptwriting, directing the actors on set, and checking how the filming looks through the camera to the final editing. Woody Allen (b. 1935) is seen here paying close attention.

SOUND

In the very early days of cinema, some film makers played gramophone records to accompany their films. But the key to 'talkies' was in having a soundtrack that was synchronized with the images.

◪ FILMING ON LOCATION

Film makers can build sets in a film studio that look just like a real street, palace, mountainside, or anything else. But often it is easier, cheaper and visually more effective to film on 'location' using the scenery and buildings of a real place. This is usually the case when a film is set in a foreign country, as with *The Last Emperor* (1987), which was filmed in China. The film makers shoot the outdoor scenes on location, and the indoor scenes in studios back home.

Television

L IKE film before it, television has had a major impact on the performing arts. Since its invention in the 1940s, television has provided thousands of new jobs for actors, directors, and all the technicians involved in the performing arts. Television has also helped to spread knowledge and understanding about all the arts – including classical music, ballet, painting, theatre and poetry – to everyone who has a television. New kinds of performing arts have been created specially for the television, such as soap operas, low-budget TV movies and pop videos. But many people will argue that television can never replace the thrill of watching the performing arts presented live and in person.

◪ COSTUME DRAMAS

Television has been able to attract audiences of millions to subjects like historical dramas by showing them in weekly episodes. 'Costume dramas', as they are called, retell in film the stories of the great classics of literature, by writers such as Thomas Hardy. Many foreign television companies broadcast the productions in translation.

◪ THE FIRST TV

The British inventor John Logie Baird (1888–1946) gave the first demonstration of a television in 1925. His apparatus included a cookie tin and darning needles. The system remained fairly basic until the 1950s. Broadcasts were in black and white, and usually performed live. Colour was introduced in 1953, but was only used widely from the 1960s.

◪ FRIENDS

TV programme makers like to produce series that they can sell to as many TV networks as possible. The American comedy *Friends* is one of the most successful ever, running to nine series since it was launched in 1994. Each actor was reported to be earning US $700,000 per episode in the final series.

VIDEO

Camcorders allow people to make their own films easily. The films have a special 'hand-held' quality that is now sometimes imitated in Hollywood movies.

▲ BRAZILIAN SOAPS

Soap operas are serialized dramas, presented regularly on television. They usually relate day-to-day dramas in the lives of ordinary people. Brazil produces a large number of soaps, called 'telenovelas', which are popular throughout the Portuguese and Spanish-speaking world. The actors are major stars in Brazil.

◄ SATELLITE

TV pictures and sound can be sent rapidly around the world. They are transmitted to satellites in stationary orbit in space, and then redirected to another part of the world. This means that live news pictures can be broadcast immediately from any trouble spots, making the world seem a smaller place.

▼ TELEVISION STUDIO

Filming for television is often done from a studio. A number of TV cameras are used at the same time. These send pictures to a control room, where the images are selected for transmission. This process has to be done very quickly for live broadcasts. The same studio may be used for a variety of programmes, so the space has to be adaptable.

lights

television camera

studio presenter

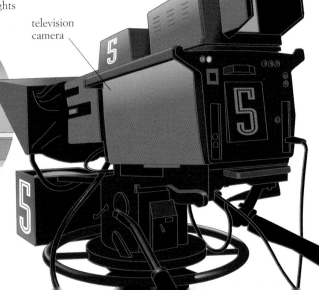

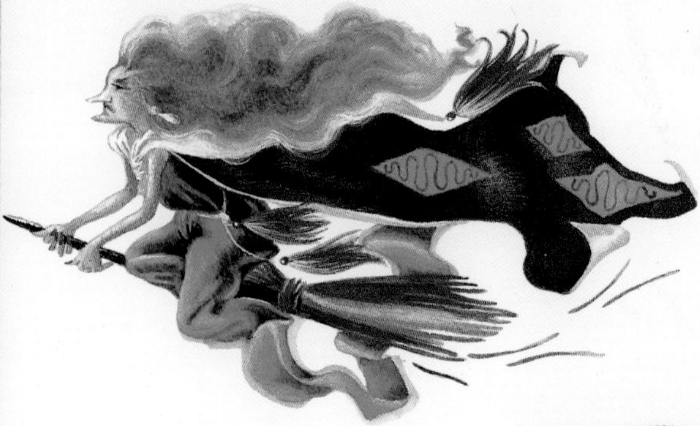

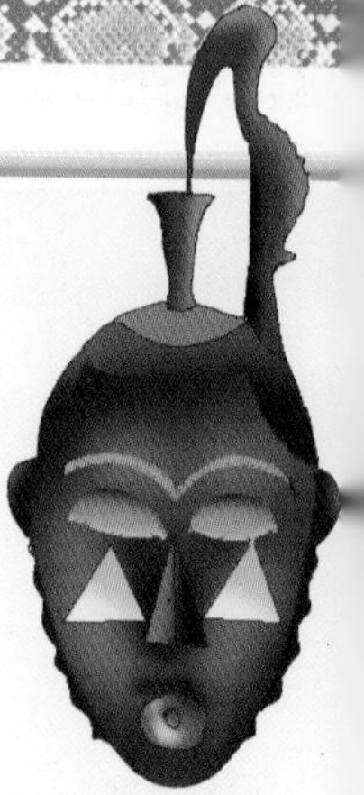

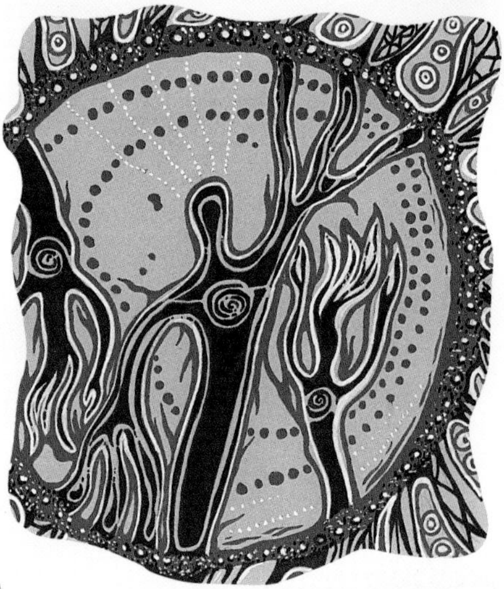

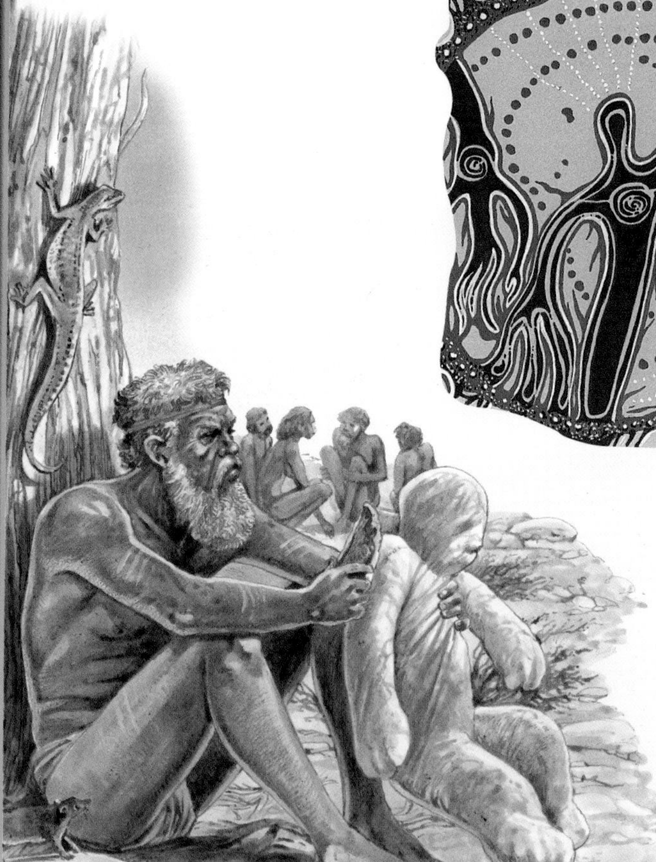

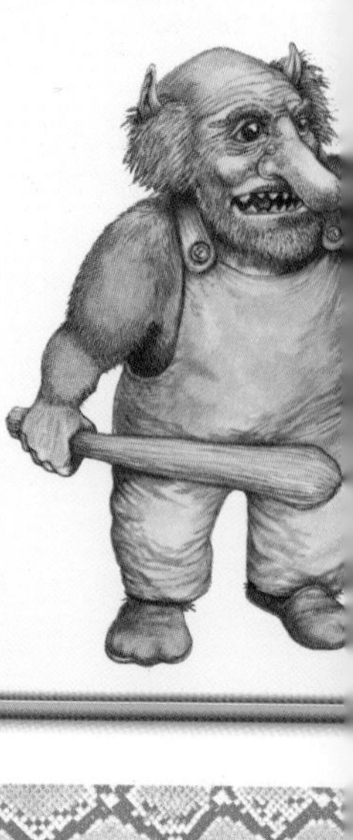

Myths and Legends

GODS and goddesses, fiends and fairies, heroes, monsters, witches and demons all play a part in myths and legends. A myth is a traditional story that tells of magical or supernatural happenings in the human world. Legends are myths linked to particular people or places. Many myths and legends are thousands of years old. At first, they were told as stories or recited as poems or songs. Later, they were written down, or told in pictures carved in wood or stone, painted on bark, stitched onto cloth or used to decorate jewellery, weapons and pots. Many of today's films and cartoons use stories and characters taken from ancient myths and legends.

Human truths

TODAY, we enjoy myths and legends because they are entertaining stories. They may amuse us, or scare us, but we do not usually believe them to be literally true. But in past centuries, myths and legends were often treated more seriously. People thought about the various 'hidden messages' they contain. Sometimes, these messages communicated deep-held religious beliefs, or gave examples of faith in action. Some myths aimed to teach moral lessons, or warn against danger. Many were designed to provide spiritual comfort, or to heal. But whatever their purpose, most contain truths about human nature which we can still learn from today.

◪ INSPIRED BY TALES

For centuries, the myths and legends of ancient times have inspired artists. Countless works of art feature mythical heroes, supernatural creatures and legendary events, like the battle scene depicted on this Greek vase (c. 350 BC).

◩ THE HOLY GRAIL

During the Middle Ages in Europe (about AD 1000 to 1500), many people believed in myths about the Holy Grail – a goblet that once held Jesus's blood. If an evil person came near it, the Grail magically disappeared. Legends told of brave knights, like King Arthur, who spent their lives searching for the Holy Grail (seen here on the Round Table).

◪ PANDORA

A Greek myth tells of the beautiful girl Pandora, sent to Earth by the gods to punish humans for daring to steal fire from heaven. She was given a splendid box, which she was told never to open. But curiosity got the better of her, and she disobeyed. All kinds of sorrows escaped from the box into the world. But right at the bottom there was Hope.

PARADISE GARDEN

In many Muslim stories, Paradise is described as a beautiful garden full of flowers, streams, and trees. Paintings showing such a garden were made for the Muslim emperors of India about AD 1600. Muslim men and women who have lived good lives hope to go to Paradise when they die.

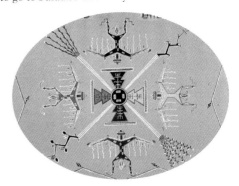

HEALING SPIRIT-PICTURE

The Navaho Native Americans create magical pictures using coloured sand. Each picture shows a scene from a myth, and depicts powerful spirits. The Navaho believe that the spirit-pictures had powers to heal.

SUN STONE

The Aztec people of Mexico carved this huge stone monument in about AD 1450. It depicts a myth that foretells the end of the world, as the Sun falls to Earth. Aztec priests made blood sacrifices on top of the stone to keep the Sun high in the sky.

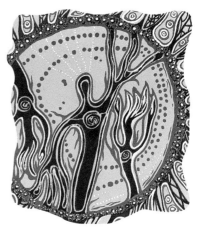

SWAMP MONSTER

Myths told by the Aborigines of Australia feature the Bunyip – a terrifying monster that lurks in creeks and swamps. Some stories suggest that the Bunyip emerges at night to seize women and children in its grasping hands and devour them.

Myths around the world

MYTHS and legends describe experiences common to people all over the world, such as finding friends, falling in love or feeling disappointed. But most are closely linked to the culture of the people who first told them. They use settings familiar to the story tellers and their audiences, and reflect a particular culture's ideas, rituals and laws. Each time the story is told, it helps to strengthen the culture's social rules. The endings of the stories often carry powerful messages about right and wrong.

◪ WITCH FROM THE WOODS

In Russia and Eastern Europe, many stories tell of the witch Baba Yaga, who flies through the air and has power over the birds and beasts. Her house in the woods stands on chickens' legs. To reach it, travellers must cross a river of fire.

◪ AFRICAN ANCESTOR MASK

In Nigeria, traditional dancers sometimes wear masks that represent powerful ancestor spirits. Many African myths tell how the spirits of dead ancestors can protect their living descendants, frighten enemies, drive out demons and keep other harmful spirits away from houses and fields.

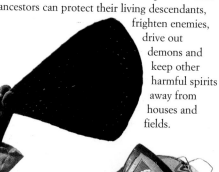

◪ RAINFOREST SPIRIT

Many legends developed about dangerous wild creatures, like this South American jaguar. To Native American peoples, it symbolized royalty and power. A hunter by night, it was linked to other nature spirits believed to roam the world after dark. Myths also told of 'were-jaguars', magical creatures that were half animal, half human.

RARE PORTRAIT OF A GOD

The Celtic peoples, whose civilization flourished in Europe from about 800 BC to AD 100, worshipped many gods. Numerous myths and legends tell of their adventures, but there are few portraits of them. This stone statue from France (c.100 BC) portrays a Celtic god holding a wild boar.

◪ A SIGN OF BELONGING

Traditionally, many New Zealand Maoris, like this warrior, decorated their skin with elaborate tattoos. The tattoo patterns were signs of adult status, bravery and clan membership. Maori legends linked living people with heroes and warriors who had died long ago.

◪ MOON SPIRIT

Carved from wood and decorated with feathers, this mask made by Inuit people from the Arctic region of North America portrays Tarqeq, the Moon spirit. Masks like this were worn by Inuit dancers, who acted out scenes from myths and legends as they danced and sang. Inuit shamans (magic healers) also wore masks, portraying spirits seen in dreams and visions.

◩ STORM GOD

Ancient legends from Japan tell the story of Susano, god of storms and seas. He was one of three children of Izanagi, the great father-god. One day, Izanagi decided to divide the world among his children, and gave all the seas to Susano. But Susano was not satisfied and quarrelled with his father, who banished him from heaven. Susano went to live in the Underworld, stealing a wife from an eight-headed dragon he met on the way.

Creation myths

HOW did we get here? Who made us? Did life evolve by accident? Or were people, animals and plants all made to fulfill a grand design? Creation myths offer answers to these important questions, usually in religious terms. They describe how gods or other supernatural forces created new worlds out of nothing, placing a sun and moon in the sky, and heaping up mountains out of the sea. In most creation myths, the gods also lay down holy laws for people to obey. The laws are often strict, but give meaning and purpose to people's lives. They reassure them that the world has a structure, and that nothing happens by chance.

☑ ADAM AND EVE

The story of Adam and Eve is told in the Bible. It tells how God created Adam, the first man, from dust. He then made Eve, the first woman, from one of Adam's ribs. When the two of them disobeyed God, he expelled them from the Garden of Eden.

☑ DREAMTIME

According to Aboriginal myths from Australia, the Dreamtime was an age long ago when Ancestor spirits roamed Earth. They shaped the landscape, showed the right way to live, and created the spirits of living creatures that would be born in future years. Today, Aboriginal people take part in religious ceremonies that allow them to join with the Dreamtime Ancestors for a while, and share in their sacred power.

☑ OLD MAN OF THE SKY

A myth from the Andes mountains of South America tells how the Inca god Wiraqocha, 'the Old Man of the Sky', created the sun, moon, and stars. Next he made statues of men and women, and brought them to life as the first humans. Then he sailed away, leaving them to make the best use of the world.

◪ IMPERIAL ANCESTOR

Amaterasu, the beautiful sun-goddess, is known in Japanese myths as 'She who makes the heavens shine'. She is also honoured as the divine ancestor of the Japanese royal family – the oldest ruling dynasty in the world today. Japanese emperors can trace their ancestry back more than 2000 years, but the legend of Amaterasu links them to a much more distant, mythical past.

◧ COSMIC EGG

Chinese myths and legends tell the amazing story of Pan Gu, the Son of Yin and Yang (the female and male forces in the universe). Pan Gu spent 18,000 years growing inside a vast cosmic egg. When he was ready to be born, he pushed the egg apart. The bottom half became Earth, and the top half formed the sky. Exhausted by his efforts, Pan Gu died. But he did not completely disappear. His breath became the wind, his voice the thunder, his eyes the sun, and moon and his hair the stars.

STAR-GODDESS

Nut was the ancient Egyptian goddess of the night sky. Her body was covered with shining stars. She was married to Geb, the earth god. Every evening, Nut swallowed the sun, and every morning she gave birth to it again at dawn.

◪ CREATOR OF OUR THOUGHTS

Hindu men and women honour Brahma as one of their three most important gods. Ancient legends tell how he continuously creates and sustains everything in the universe as he meditates, or thinks deeply, about holy things. As the god of wisdom, he creates all the thoughts that come into people's minds. He is often portrayed with four faces, to show that he sees and knows everything.

Animal myths

FOR many thousands of years, people were more closely involved with animals than they are today. They hunted them for their meat and skins, milked them, tamed them to provide transport or kept them as pets. Recognizing that each kind of animal had special characteristics, they invented myths and legends about them. Some explained, for example, why lions were brave, or why bees worked so hard. Others told of the differences between animals and humans, and explained why humans claimed the right to control all other living things. Many animals were sacred to the gods and heroes – legends told how the animals helped them, guarded them, and shared in their adventures.

◣ UNICORN

Unicorns are described in many myths and legends. They have the body of a horse, the feet of a deer, a goatlike beard and a single, twisted horn. Often, they are symbols of purity and spiritual healing.

◣ THE THROTTLER

The ancient Greek Sphinx (the name means 'throttler') was a cruel monster with a woman's face and chest, a lion's body and tail and a bird's wings. It lay in wait for travellers outside the city of Thebes, refusing to let them pass until they had answered a puzzling riddle. Anyone who failed to give the right answer was killed by the sphinx – the ground beneath its perch was littered with human bones.

◣ HELL HOUND

Ancient Greek and Roman legends tell of Cerberus, a three-headed dog who guarded the entrance to the Underworld. His tail was like a snake, and poisonous flowers sprouted where his saliva fell. Although Cerberus welcomed all dead souls, he became fierce if they tried to escape back to Earth.

◻ SPIDER MONKEY

Impressive trees and mountains and characterful animals have often inspired myths and legends. The treetop antics of spider monkeys, for example, feature in many traditional stories told by the Maya people from the rainforests of Central and South America. Some of the oldest Maya stories describe the adventures of a pair of hero twins, named Xbalanque and Hunahpu, who turned their brother into a monkey because he was stealing their food.

◻ THUNDERBIRD

Typically, traditional stories from around the world give a recognizable shape to frightening, invisible forces such as storms, winds and rain. Myths and legends told by Native North American peoples describe the Thunderbird – a mighty creature like an eagle that rides on the winds. Lightning flashes from its eyes, the beating of its wings sounds like thunder, and it is so big that it can carry a whale in its talons.

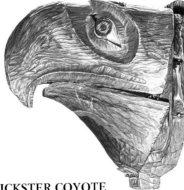

ELEPHANT GOD

Ganesh is a helpful Hindu god. People pray to him when they face difficulties, or before setting off on a journey. Legends tell how Ganesh was born with a human head. But his father, the god Shiva, cut it off, and replaced it with the head of an elephant.

◻ TRICKSTER COYOTE

Many Native American myths involve the coyote, a wily trickster who is also tricked. The Native American peoples believe the coyote to possess characteristics that are decidely human – and these lead to him having good as well as bad experiences.

Myths of place and time

CURIOSITY about our surroundings is a powerful human instinct. Dramatic landscapes – particularly mountains, forests, and deserts – inspire feelings of awe, and sometimes, sheer terror. People are also intrigued by regular patterns in time – the changing seasons, for example, or sunrise and sunset. They ask how did they begin, and when will they end? All these feelings are reflected in myths about place and time. Some feature natural wonders, some tell how a civilization began, and some try to explain natural phenomena such as rainbows.

◪ ROMULUS AND REMUS

According to a Roman legend, the city of Rome was founded in 753 BC by Romulus and Remus – twin boys who were abandoned at birth and adopted by a wolf. Later, during a quarrel, Romulus killed Remus, and went on to build the city alone, so it was named after him. Eventually Rome ruled a vast empire.

◪ LAND OF YOUTH

A famous Celtic legend tells the story of Oisin, an Irish prince who was befriended by the goddess Niamh. She carried him away to Tir Nan Og – the mythical Land of Youth, where no one ever grew old. But Oisin soon felt lonely there, and asked Niamh to let him go. When he returned to Earth, everything had changed. He could not find his home or his family. Without knowing it, he had been in Tir Nan Og for 300 years.

◪ DREAM PICTURE

About AD 1200, the Aztecs of northern Mexico left their homeland and moved south. In a dream, their leader was shown where to build their new capital city, Tenochtitlan. He was to build it where he saw an eagle sitting on a cactus eating a snake.

LOST CITY OF ATLANTIS

An ancient Greek myth described a prosperous island-city called Atlantis, lying to the west of Greece. One day, without warning, the island-city vanished beneath the waves. Archaeologists think that the myth of Atlantis was based on a real event – a massive volcanic eruption that demolished most of the island of Thera (now Santorini) in about 1400 BC.

LAND OF GOLD

El Dorado was a mythical country in South America. Many travellers claimed that it was rich in gold, and ruled over by a golden king. During the 16th and 17th centuries, explorers from Spain set out to find it and make their fortunes. But they all failed, and some died.

RAINBOW BRIDGE

Many Viking myths feature a beautiful rainbow bridge, named Bifrost, that linked Midgard (Earth) with Asgard (heaven, the home of the gods). The bridge was guarded by a powerful god named Heimdall. When enemies approached, he summoned help by blowing his magic horn.

A HOLY PLACE

For thousands of years, Uluru (also known as Ayers Rock) in central Australia has been a holy place for Aboriginal people. They hold religious ceremonies there to make contact with ancestor spirits from the Dreamtime. Uluru features in many Aboriginal myths and legends.

Myths that teach

MYTHS and legends are full of traditional wisdom, told in an entertaining way. Some contain hidden warnings, designed to keep unruly members of society under control. Others aim to strengthen people's feelings of loyalty to their nation by explaining how traditional customs developed. In Germany during World War II (1939–45), Nazi leaders invented false legends that encouraged Germanic peoples to believe they were a 'master race', destined to rule the world. Like myths and legends, fairy stories also teach in an entertaining way. Based on folk tales, some warn what might happen if children stray from home, or tell lies.

◤ QUEEN OF ELFLAND

In the Scottish legend 'Tam Lin', a young man named Tam is captured by the Queen of Elfland. But his girlfriend Janet refuses to let him go. Brave and determined, she holds fast to Tam as the Queen changes him into a succession of terrifying monsters. Finally, the Queen sets Tam free.

◤ BEAUTY AND THE BEAST

Written in Italy about AD 1500, *Beauty and the Beast* is a story of love and trust. Beauty, a young girl, agrees to marry the Beast because he has promised to help her father. She is scared of him at first, but also feels sorry for him and treats him kindly. Her love is rewarded when the Beast turns into a handsome prince.

◤ GODDESS OF DISEASES

Ancient Egyptian people feared the lion-headed goddess Sekhmet, whom they believed brought terrible diseases to the world. Myths and legends taught that illnesses were sent by the gods to punish people, and to warn them to behave better in future.

☑ AESOP'S FABLES

Stories with a moral message, known as 'fables', have been popular for thousands of years. Some of the best known were collected by Aesop (c. 600 BC), a slave in ancient Greece. His fable of the fox and the stork warns people not to be boastful.

STORM WARNINGS

Sailors created myths to pass on their knowledge of weather forecasting. One featured a mythical old mother – the Moon – who lived in the sky. Mother Carey's chickens were storm petrels – seabirds that sailors believed could forecast storms.

☑ FIGHTING FOR GOLD

Siegfried is the hero of many myths and legends from Germany and Scandinavia. In a famous battle, he fought and killed the dragon Fafnir, who guarded a magnificent hoard of gold. But the hoard contained a ring that was cursed to bring death to anyone who owned it – including Siegfried. His story is a warning that wealth is not the source of happiness, and can be dangerous.

☑ SPIDER STORIES

Myths and traditional tales from many parts of the world feature spiders or spider webs. Some of the best-known spider stories come from West Africa and the Caribbean. They describe the adventures of Anansi, a clever, cunning spider – and are an encouragement to children to be quick witted.

Myths that inspire

FOR centuries, people have told myths and legends about powerful gods and spirits, as a way of explaining mysterious or frightening events around them. The stories also put into words people's hopes and fears. Religious leaders from different faiths tell 'parables' – stories containing examples of good and bad behaviour, which encourage believers to choose the right way to live. Many myths are inspiring – wicked monsters are defeated by brave heroes and heroines, and lonely people find true love. These stories encourage the listener to believe that, one day, good will triumph over evil, and that honest, kind, faithful people will be rewarded with happiness.

◳ MOSES

The Bible story of Moses has inspired Jewish people for more than 3000 years. It tells how Moses led the Jews out of Egypt, where they had been slaves. The Jews believed that Moses was guided by God, and that he would lead them to the Promised Land. On the way, in the wilderness, at God's command Moses gave the people water by striking a rock with his staff.

◱ FAITHFUL DEVOTION

Sati was the wife of Lord Shiva, one of the three main Hindu gods. She was famous for her loyalty and devotion to her husband. Legends tell how she burned herself alive on his funeral pyre, or bonfire, as a sacrifice. In the past, widows in India were urged to follow Sati's example. The custom was banned in 1829.

◲ WISE LEADER

Many legends are told about Siddhartha Gautama, an Indian prince (563–483 BC). As a young man, he left his home and family and spent years in study and meditation. He became known as the Buddha – the Enlightened One – because of his great wisdom. Many people (Buddhists) follow his example.

◨ WARRIOR SAINT

Joan of Arc was born in northern France in 1412. As a young peasant girl, she began to hear voices, which she believed came from heaven. The voices told Joan to help lead the French troops against the English, who were trying to conquer French lands. Joan's faith and courage inspired many French soldiers, but she was captured, put on trial and executed by the English in 1431. Later, the Roman Catholic Church made her a saint.

◪ SERVANT OF GOD

St. Francis (1182–1226) is one of the most inspiring Christian saints. He left his wealthy home in Assisi, Italy, to live as a beggar. With his followers, he helped the poor and preached about God's love to all creation, including the birds and animals.

◪ IMMORTALS

Chinese people who followed the ancient Daoist philosophy honoured the Immortals – eight supernatural beings who had discovered a magical elixir of life that allowed them to live forever. The Immortals had special powers, such as becoming invisible, bringing dead people back to life or turning objects into gold.

NATIONAL HERO?

In Switzerland, William Tell is a national hero. But was he real or just a myth? The story goes that as a punishment for disobeying the Austrians, who ruled Switzerland, he was made to shoot an arrow at an apple balanced on his son's head. Today, scholars think he never existed.

Myths that amuse

LAUGHTER adds zest to life. So it is not surprising that many traditional myths and legends feature a joker or trickster – a bold, playful character who tells strange stories and makes the audience laugh. The trickster's jokes and games often have a purpose – such as rescuing a hero from trouble. Mostly we laugh along with the heroes or villains, and share in their fun. But in some traditional tales, humour is used in a sharper, less kindly way. Jokes are told that ridicule unpopular characters and make them look stupid. In such tales, laughter is used as a powerful weapon of attack.

☑ TREACHEROUS TROLL

Wizened, hairy and clever, trolls are often amusing, but they can also be treacherous, mischievous and cruel. They feature in many ancient myths and legends from Scandinavia. Traditionally, trolls live deep inside hills and mountains, and are expert metalworkers. They love gold and treasure, and hate noise.

◥ FRIGHTENINGLY FUNNY

Over the centuries, many sinister figures from traditional myths and legends have been turned into pleasant or harmless characters, suitable for children's films or picture books. For example, the American movie *Hocus Pocus*, made in 1993, features three silly, clumsy witches, who are very funny and not particularly frightening. They are outwitted by a group of children.

◰ SATYRS

The ancient Greeks and Romans enjoyed watching comic plays about satyrs – mythical forest creatures that were part man, part horse, with horns like a goat. Wild, rude and full of energy, satyrs were often pictured drinking with Bacchus, the Roman god of wine.

◻ THE UGLY SISTERS

Two scheming, ugly sisters feature in *Cinderella* – one of Europe's best-known traditional tales about a poor servant girl, a fairy godmother, a prince and a glass slipper. It was first written down in France in about 1650. Cinderella's story is often performed as a pantomime, with the roles of the two ugly sisters played as comic parts by men. In the end the sisters are punished for their harsh treatment of Cinderella by seeing her marry the prince.

◪ BRER RABBIT

Stories about wily Brer Rabbit (Brother Rabbit) outwitting his great enemy, Brer Fox, were first published in 1879. Author Joel Chandler Harris may have been inspired by traditional tales told by African Americans living in his native South.

◪ ALADDIN

Aladdin summons a genie – a powerful spirit – by rubbing his magic lamp. With the genie's help, he escapes from poverty, marries the king of China's daughter, and builds a great palace in Africa. The story of Aladdin is just one of many tales full of magic and mystery that were collected about AD 1400 in the Middle East. Today, they are known as 'Tales from the Arabian Nights'.

CRUEL TRICKSTER

Son of a giant and father of monsters, Loki was the Viking god of trouble and strife. His tricks could be amusing, but they angered the other gods so much that they chained Loki to a rock, where he will remain a prisoner forever.

Myths that entertain

PEOPLE have always enjoyed listening to myths about famous explorers, terrifying monsters, or magical other-worlds. Centuries ago, the tales were handed down by word of mouth. Later, they were written down in books, or performed as plays and ballets. Today, bloody historical epics, scary horror stories and romantic tales of love are made into movies or shown on TV. If a myth or legend is well told, it stimulates the imagination and provides an escape from everyday life.

◪ GREEDY GIANT

Big, stupid, clumsy, and greedy giants feature in myths and legends from many parts of the world. In some stories they represent uncontrollable forces of nature, such as earthquakes or thunder. In others they embody feelings of rage or jealousy.

◪ GISELLE

A German legend tells the story of a beautiful girl, Giselle, who falls in love with Albrecht, a man who loves someone else. Heartbroken, she flees to live with the ghosts of women who died before their wedding day. Together, they try to kill Albrecht by making him dance until he drops dead.

◪ FILM MONSTER

Godzilla is a mighty lizard-like monster (right). Created in Japan in 1954, he starred in many films, fighting aliens and robots, and defending planet Earth from genetically engineered monsters.

◄ RIDERS IN THE SKY

The Valkyries were twelve Viking goddesses who served the great god Odin. They charged into battle with him armed with swords, and flew above the fighting men, choosing who would live and who would die. The Valkyries carried the dead warriors back with them to Valhalla, a palace in heaven, where they feasted and drank forever.

EVIL QUEEN

Dancers and musicians on Bali, Indonesia, tell the story of the evil queen Rangda. Based on the real-life wicked ruler Queen Mahendradatta, who lived almost a thousand years ago, Rangda is portrayed as a ragged witch with long hair and spiky nails.

◄ SINGING A STORY

Griots are traditional singers and storytellers from West Africa. They entertain crowds in busy streets and market places, and also sing in people's homes. Many of their songs recall events in local history, and the deeds of famous kings and queens. Griots pass on their special knowledge to their children. In places where many people cannot read and write, griot songs are an important way of preserving information about the past.

◄ OPERA HERO

Sigurd, also known as Siegfried, is the hero of many ancient legends from Germany and Scandinavia. He is also the hero of several 19th-century operas by German composer Richard Wagner. In both, Sigurd wields a magic sword, rides a supernatural horse and is able to understand the words that birds sing.

Heroes and history

SOME of the most exciting and enjoyable myths and legends tell of the adventures of brave heroes who fight against wicked villains, or recount epic journeys across mountains, deserts and seas in search of new homes or promised lands. Often, myths describe how gods and goddesses help specially favoured people, such as the Roman hero Aeneas. He was guided by the gods toward a new homeland in Italy. Aeneas was an imaginary figure. But some historical myths record the deeds of kings and queens who actually existed. They became so famous in their lifetimes that stories about them continued to be told long after they were dead.

◥ INDIAN EPIC HERO

Rama is the hero of the Indian epic *Ramayana*. He is regarded as the perfect man, husband, brother, king and obedient son, and is charged with the task of killing the demon king, Ravana.

◥ NOBLE KNIGHT

Sir Perceval (or 'Parsifal') was one of the Knights of the Round Table – 200 brave, noble soldiers who served King Arthur, legendary king of Britain. Stories tell how their meeting table was round, so that no man could sit at its head and feel superior to the others. Even though King Arthur and his knights probably never existed, their story was very popular in Europe during the Middle Ages (c. AD 1000–1500).

◥ ODYSSEUS THE WANDERER

According to Greek legend, Odysseus was king of Ithaca. He fought in the long war between Greece and Troy (now in Turkey). But on his way home, his ship was wrecked and he spent ten years wandering – surviving many adventures before reaching home. When he returned home, only his wife and dog recognized him.

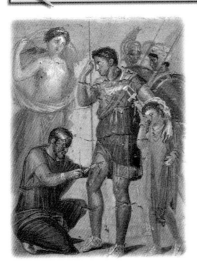

◤ BOLD PRINCE AENEAS

Aeneas was forced into exile after the city of Troy was destroyed by war. He fled to North Africa, where he fell in love with Queen Dido. But dreams warned him that his destiny lay elsewhere. He sailed to Italy and settled near Rome, where his descendants later became rulers.

HOLY HERO

In myths told by West African peoples, the hero Ogun (also known as Gu) was the son of the great Creator Twins. He was sent to Earth to help humans by teaching them how to work iron and make tools, so that they could build houses and farm the land. Ogun is one of many mythical heroes who link gods and people.

◪ STRONG MAN

The hero Hercules was admired by the ancient Greeks for his great strength. But he could also be vicious, so the god Apollo punished him by setting him twelve 'labours', or tasks, to complete. These included killing the Hydra, a multi-headed snake whose heads regrew each time they were cut off.

◪ SON OF A GOD

Cuchulainn was the son of an Irish princess and the Celtic god Lugh. He was taught how to fight by a witch, who gave him a deadly barbed spear. Cuchulainn led the Men of Ulster on countless raids, and fought many battles single-handed. Eventually he was killed when the goddess Bodhbh, in the form of a raven, helped his enemies trap him.

Myths that warn

WHY do bad things happen to people? Over the centuries, storytellers have created myths and legends that try to explain the causes of sorrow and suffering. Often, the stories blame misfortunes on human wickedness, and contain powerful warnings of what might happen to people who ignore the gods, or disobey society's rules. Other myths blame evil creatures from the supernatural world, and warn humans against meddling with them. A few also feature kindly spirits, such as angels, who bring wise warnings to humankind.

◤ DEADLY BEAUTY

Actaeon was a hunter in ancient Greece. Legends tell how, one day in the woods, he met the goddess Artemis bathing in a pool with her companions. Struck by her beauty, he stopped to spy on her. Outraged, the goddess turned Actaeon into a stag, and his own dogs chased and killed him. The story warned Greek men and women to treat their gods and goddesses with respect – and fear.

◤ ANGEL VOICES

Angels are described as 'messengers from God' in Jewish, Christian, and Muslim holy texts. Some angels bring good news, while others warn of dangers. The Angel Raphael, for example, told Adam to obey God, or risk losing Paradise. Usually angels appear in visions or dreams.

◤ SEA MONSTERS

A triton is a kind of sea monster. According to some Greek myths, the first triton was a merman, with a human head and a sea-serpent's tail. But in later legends, tritons have pointed noses, hairy heads, wide mouths with sharp teeth, scaly bodies, and dolphin's tails. They could calm storms at sea and control the waves.

◻ APPROACHING DEATH

Banshees were fairy-women who haunted the Celtic countries of northern Europe, warning men, women, and children of approaching death. They announced their presence with an eerie wail, usually at night. Anyone who heard the sound believed that they would soon die. Another Celtic doom-spirit appeared by rivers washing bloody clothes. Any man who saw her as he was setting off to battle knew he would die.

◻ SEEKING A SPIRIT WARNING

Among Native peoples of North America, and in parts of northern Asia, shamans – magic healers – danced, chanted, drank potions and performed rituals as ways of making contact with the spirit world. They hoped their own spirit would travel there, and learn wisdom or receive warnings from the spirit powers.

BIRD WISDOM

For almost 1000 years, ravens have lived at the Tower of London. The Tower's guardians believe that if the ravens ever leave, disaster will follow. This superstition may have arisen from the fact that ravens are sensitive to bad weather – their leaving might warn of approaching storms.

◻ GHOSTLY VISION

People from many different cultures believe that ghosts can bring messages from beyond the grave. Some myths suggest ghosts warn of future dangers so that people can avoid them. Others warn sinners to improve their behaviour or face a terrible punishment after death.

Mythical monsters

IN MYTHS and legends, the word 'monster' means
something that is scary, sinister, or huge in size.
Monsters can be clever or foolish, but they are always
unpleasant, and often dangerous. Some monsters, such
as the Norwegian 'maelstrom' (man-eating whirlpool),
represent wild natural forces that cannot be controlled.
Others flesh out terrors, such as fear of the dark, that
have haunted humans for thousands of years. Meeting
monsters safely in stories, plays and movies helps people
to confront their fears, and survive. Most monsters are
imaginary. But sometimes the word 'monster' is used to
describe violent criminals or wartime enemies. It shows
how 'inhuman' we think their behaviour is.

◪ FRANKENSTEIN'
MONSTER

Created by writer Mary
Shelley in 1818,
Frankenstein's monster
was made from dead
corpses joined together.
At first friendly, it
turned violent and
began to kill people.
Frankenstein blamed
himself for meddling
with nature.

◪ MAGICAL MERMAID
MONSTERS

According to German legend,
monsters shaped like beautiful
women, called Lorelei,
sat on jagged rocks in
the Rhine River. They
spent their days
combing their
hair and singing
enchanting songs.
But fishermen who
were drawn to the
magical music
met certain
death in the
fast-flowing
waters or
on the
rocks.

◪ MINOTAUR

The Minotaur was a
monster of ancient
Greek legend. It had
the body of a man,
but the head, horns,
and tail of a bull, and
it fed on human flesh.
The Minotaur was kept in a labyrinth – a
maze of twisting passages – beneath the
palace of King Minos of Crete. It was killed
by the hero-prince Theseus, who found his
way through the maze and back again by
leaving a trail of thread behind him.

CENTAURS

Centaurs were legendary wild creatures that lived in the forests of ancient Greece. Half man and half horse, they fed on raw flesh and were driven wild by the sight of women or the smell of wine. Centaurs were sworn enemies of the Greeks, who prided themselves on their civilized behaviour and self-control.

SUSQUATCH

Many hunters in North American forests have reported seeing the Susquatch or Bigfoot – a huge, hairy monster rather like an ape, but bigger and stronger than a man. No clear Bigfoot tracks or bodies have ever been found. But in 1967 two men shot some film of an apelike creature at Bluff Creek, California. Is it evidence that Bigfoot exists, or is it a fake?

FIERY PHOENIX

The Phoenix was a magical bird that lived for 500 years without eating or drinking. It lived in the deserts of the Middle East, in a nest of sweet-smelling twigs and herbs. When the time came for it to die, it set fire to itself. But it was reborn from its own ashes after three days, ready to live again.

BLOODTHIRSTY VAMPIRES

There are many stories of vampires – dead bodies that have returned to life. By day they look like ordinary men or women, though they cast no shadow and make no reflection in mirrors. But at night they grow wings like bats, their teeth change into fangs, and they drink the blood of living people to survive. The most famous vampire was Count Dracula, said to live in a castle in Transylvania, in Romania.

MOKELE-MBENDE

The Mokele-Mbende looks like a dinosaur. It is reported to live in swamps in West Africa, where conditions are similar to those of 65 million years ago, when dinosaurs were alive. Scientists have found footprints, but no firm evidence that this 'living dinosaur' survives.

Myths of doom

EVEN today, in the 21st century, we do not know when our lives will end. We cannot be sure that our homes and families will stay secure, or that our nation will remain peaceful. In the past, life was even more uncertain. So myths and legends about doom and disaster helped people face up to their feelings of anxiety, loss, and fear. But other myths were positive and offered hope for the future. They promised that even if this world came to an end, it would be re-born, better and more beautiful.

◪ GHOST SHIP

Sailors travelling around the dangerous Cape of Good Hope – the southern tip of Africa – told many stories about the 'Flying Dutchman'. Some said it was a ghost ship that lured real vessels into danger. Others said the 'Dutchman' was a ghostly sea captain who had been wicked while he lived, and was being punished by being made to sail the seas forever.

◪ HUNGRY AT THE FEAST

King Midas ruled Phrygia (now in Turkey). He was rich and powerful, but rather stupid. Always greedy for treasure, Midas asked the Greek god Dionysus to give him the magic power to turn anything he touched into gold. Dionysus agreed, but Midas soon found that even food and drink became solid metal the moment they reached his mouth. His greed meant that he was doomed to starve.

◪ SIBYL'S CAVE

Sibyl of Cumae, in Italy, was a wise woman who lived in a cave. Inspired by the gods, she was able to see into the future. The god Apollo promised her anything she wanted, so she asked to live for a thousand years. But she forgot to ask to stay young. Gradually, she withered and grew so small that she had to be kept in a bottle in her own cave.

DEIRDRE OF THE SORROWS

Deirdre was the beautiful, tragic heroine of many Irish legends. She was doomed from birth to bring death and misery. To prevent this, the king of Ireland kept her prisoner. But Deirdre escaped with the man she loved.

RAGNAROK

According to Viking myths, Ragnarok – the Twilight of the Gods – was a terrible day of doom, when the old world and all things living there perished. In a final battle between good and evil, even the gods were killed. But a wonderful new world was created from the ruins to start living again.

THE END OF THE WORLD

In the Christian Bible, St. John predicts that the 'Four Horsemen of the Apocalypse' – who represent war, famine, plague and death – will appear with many other terrifying creatures as the world comes to an end. But he has faith that Jesus will return to rule over a glorious kingdom forever.

PIED PIPER

The legend of the Pied Piper tells how, in 1284, a mysterious piper rid the town of Hamelin in Germany of its plague of rats. When he played his pipe, all the rats followed him to their deaths. But the townsfolk refused to pay the piper. So he played again, and this time all the children followed him out of the town. They were never seen again.

Modern myths

FOR the past 200 years, science has provided us with vast amounts of new and exciting information. It has also offered us explanations of many things that formerly seemed mysterious, and were the subject of myths and legends – from the Sun and the stars to the workings of the human mind. But in spite of this knowledge, myths and legends have not disappeared. In fact, they are still being created today. Some contain valuable truths. Others are based on false hopes, fears, and fantasies. But like traditional tales, modern myths still have the power to capture our imagination and make us think.

◣ PERFECTION?

Many myths feature characters who represent perfect beauty. Today, their myth is kept alive by fashion designers, who choose exceptionally tall, slim and beautiful young women, like German-born supermodel Claudia Schiffer, to model their clothes. They offer a standard of beauty few can hope to achieve.

◣ JAWS!

Left undisturbed, most wild creatures are unlikely to attack humans. But there are many mythical stories about 'man-eating' creatures, especially sharks and tigers. Some of the stories are true. Sharks are known to attack bathers, as shown in the thriller film *Jaws*.

◻ HEROES OR VILLAINS?

Bonnie Parker and Clyde Barrow were violent gangsters who killed many innocent victims before being shot by police in 1934. Before long, legends grew up about them, celebrating their courage and defiance. And in 1967, their mythical status increased when they were portrayed as romantic, glamorous freedom-fighters in a popular Hollywood movie.

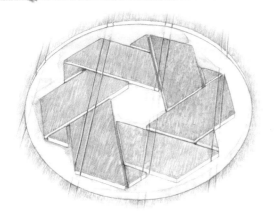

◄ CROP CIRCLES

Since the 1980s, mysterious patterns have appeared in fields of wheat in Europe and North America. Known as 'crop circles' – though they may be any shape—they have puzzled many farmers and expert investigators. The patterns are made by crushing the crop in particular areas. But no one knows for certain who or what has made them – plant disease, jokers, or even aliens!

SPACE RACE HEROES

During the 1960s, the United States and the USSR both hoped to be the first nation to land a human on the Moon. Astronauts like Neil Armstrong became national heroes, with the characteristics of legendary heroes from the past.

◄ SUPERSTAR

American actor Brad Pitt is one of the most popular film stars of modern times. Newspapers often encourage readers to think that the lives of such superstars are as dramatic as the mythical characters they portray on screen.

◄ CLINTONS – IMAGE OR REALITY?

Politicians the world over—including former president Bill Clinton—take great care to display a particular public image. Experts known as 'spin doctors' help them to present their characters, policies and achievements in the most positive ways. But politicians are often accused of hiding the truth behind false myths.

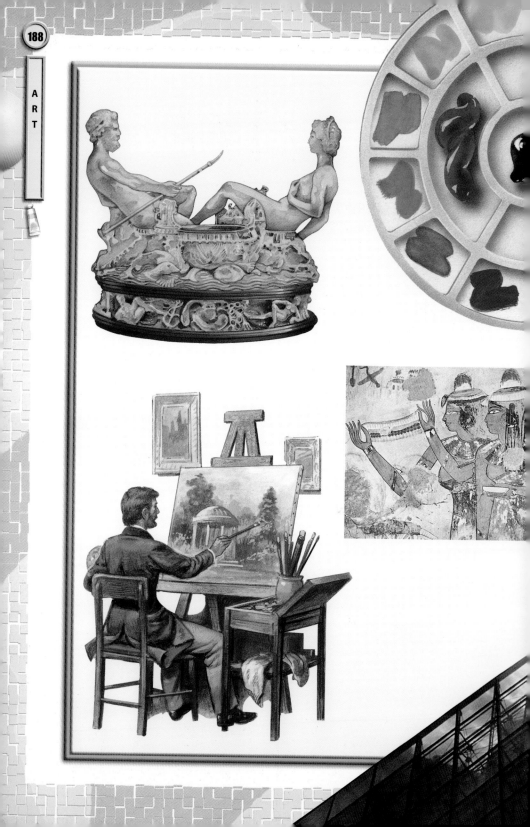

Art

EVERYONE has a favourite piece of art. It could be a painting you have at home, or a print of a famous painting by one of the great artists of the past. Or it could be a photograph in a book, or a sculpture in a park. There is something about that work of art that appeals to you in a special way, and makes you remember it. Art is about creating visual images, reordering dollops of paint or a block of stone to produce something memorable. But art is more than simply something to look at and admire. It represents the personal vision of the artist, and offers a channel of communication between the artist and the viewer. Over the centuries, ideas about how this should be done have changed, providing us with an extraordinary historical record of the changing ways people have viewed the world.

Painting as decoration

ANY thousands of years before the very first civilizations developed in Mesopotamia, Egypt and China, artists had begun to decorate the world in which they lived. We know this because paintings have been found on the walls of caves dating back to at least 18,000 BC. Painting is clearly a natural instinct of human beings. There are many reasons why artists paint, but one is to make our surroundings look more interesting, more personal and more beautiful.

ROMAN MURAL

The Romans liked to decorate the insides of their houses with wall paintings, or 'murals'. Many murals were found in excellent condition in Pompeii – a Roman city near Naples that was buried under tonnes of ash when the volcano Vesuvius erupted in AD 79.

ETHIOPIAN WALL PAINTING

Ethiopia was the first country in Africa to adopt Christianity, in AD 321, and ever since artists have painted the interior walls of its churches with murals. The brightly coloured pictures show figures from the Bible and later Christian saints.

THE LASCAUX CAVE PAINTINGS

In 1940, four French boys were searching for treasure in a cave near the Dordogne River in southwest France when they discovered some amazing prehistoric cave paintings. Made over 15,000 years ago, the paintings depict animals such as bison, deer, and horses.

☐ MINOAN MURALS

The Minoan civilization developed on Crete and neighbouring Mediterranean islands from about 2200 BC, but collapsed after about 1100 BC. In recent years, archaeologists have unearthed a number of Minoan palaces, such as Knossos on Crete, and have found the remains of many colourful and lively murals that adorned their walls. This one is of a tree blowing in the wind.

◪ TRICKING THE EYE – *TROMPE L'OEIL*

By imitating stone and marble surfaces, and using clever shading techniques, artists discovered that they could transform a plain, flat wall into a convincing architectural feature, which appeared to have depth. Here, the Italian artist Paolo Veronese (1528–88) has created a country scene, viewed through an elaborate painted stone arch.

☑ MEXICAN MURALS

Wall paintings and mosaics (made of thousands of tiny glass-coated tiles) are sometimes used to decorate the outsides of buildings. The tradition is particularly strong in Mexico, as seen here at Mexico City University. Most old murals are found on inside walls, mainly because murals on outside walls are gradually destroyed by the weather.

POTTERY

It is not just walls that are decorated with paintings. Since ancient times, pottery has been beautifully painted with patterns and pictures, ranging from simple geometric designs to elaborate and complex scenes, including figures and landscapes.

Religious art

THE history of art is closely linked to religion. Painting was used to decorate places of worship, such as Buddhist and Hindu temples and Christian churches. This was partly to make them the most attractive places in the community, as a way of showing respect and reverence for the gods. But it was also a way of teaching worshippers about stories from the scriptures – especially useful in the days when not many people could read. Religious communities were often wealthy, and could pay for the best artists of the day to work for them.

◥ ILLUMINATED MANUSCRIPT

In medieval Europe, most books were produced by Christian monks. They wrote the books out by hand, and illustrated them with colourful paintings, called 'illuminations'. Many of the early skills of European painting were learned through manuscript illumination.

◥ EGYPTIAN TOMB PAINTING

The ancient Egyptians decorated the inside walls of their tombs with elaborate paintings depicting the lives of the dead. This was a way of affirming their belief that the dead person would continue to lead a similar life in the afterworld. Faces are always shown with the head turned sideways, 'in profile'.

◤ TIBETAN TANKA

Buddhist temple hangings from Tibet are known as 'tankas'. Painted onto canvas following strict rules, they show gods, holy beings, and sacred symbols. The images are considered sacred, and are designed to help worshipers pray. Here, the 11th-century saint Milarepa is seen surrounded by his disciples.

GIOTTO

One of the great early European painters was the Italian Giotto di Bodone (c.1267–1337). He decorated the walls of the Scrovegni Chapel in Padua with a series of scenes from the life of Christ. In *The Raising of Lazarus*, Christ is seen bringing the dead Lazarus back to life.

MUSLIM PATTERNS

In Islam, it is forbidden to paint pictures of people or animals. So artists decorate the mosques and holy books with beautiful and intricate geometric patterns.

ICONS

Icons are sacred images, usually painted on wood, made for the Christian Orthodox Church. They show figures from the Christian scriptures and saints. The two saints in this 16th-century icon founded a monastery in Russia. Icons are believed to provide a precious channel of communication between worshippers and God.

STAINED GLASS

In medieval times, Christian churches were the grandest buildings in Europe, filled with paintings and treasures. Colored, or 'stained'. glass windows were decorated with scenes from the Bible. The art of making stained glass is still practiced today, adding dramatic colour to modern churches.

Renaissance painting

AFTER about 1300, great changes in art came about in Italy. Artists, sculptors, architects and scholars began to rediscover the genius of the ancient Greek and Roman civilizations. This period of rediscovery became known as the Renaissance (French for 'rebirth'). It lasted for over two centuries, gradually spreading throughout Europe. During the Renaissance, artists discovered new ways of copying the real world more accurately.

◻ OIL PAINTING

Oil painting was developed in northern Europe after about 1400. The oil allowed artists to blend their colours smoothly, and to show the delicate effect of light through gentle shading. As a result, figures became more three-dimensional, as in this Madonna and Child by Italian artist Giovanni Bellini (1430–1516).

◪ PERSPECTIVE

During the Renaissance, for the first time artists became aware of the rules of 'perspective', which allow three-dimensional space to be shown realistically in a flat painting. They realized that things appear smaller the farther away they are, and that the parallel lines of buildings point towards a 'vanishing point' – as in this painting by Domenico di Bartolo (c.1400–44).

◪ RUBENS

Italy remained the great centre for European art throughout the Renaissance. Artists from northern Europe went there to learn, including Flemish painter Pieter-Paul Rubens (1577–1640), famous for his lively works.

☑ CARAVAGGIO

Oil paint allowed artists to create the colours of very deep, dark shadows, as well as strong or subtle light effects – a technique known as chiaroscuro (meaning 'light-dark'). The great master of chiaroscuro was the Italian Michelangelo Merisi da Caravaggio (1571–1610). His *Supper at Emmaus* depicts Christ's reappearance after the Crucifixion.

▨ BOTTICELLI

In medieval times, most art was paid for by the Church. But during the Renaissance, wealthy rulers became patrons of the arts. This meant that artists could paint new subjects that were not religious, such as portraits, battle scenes and pictures from Greek and Roman mythology. A famous example is the *Birth of Venus* (the Roman goddess of love) by the Italian Sandro Botticelli (c.1444–1510).

▨ HOLBEIN

One of the greatest portrait painters of the Renaissance was the German artist Hans Holbein the Younger (c.1497–1543). He painted many of the most famous people of his times in minute detail, including King Henry VIII of England, shown here. Holbein lived in England after 1532.

THE GENIUS OF LEONARDO DA VINCI

The greatest Renaissance artists were not just painters and sculptors, but also gifted architects, engineers, poets, and musicians. One of the most famous is the Italian Leonardo da Vinci (1452–1519). Although celebrated as a painter, he only completed about 25 paintings. He spent much of his time making drawings of his inventions – such as this flying machine, multi-barrelled guns, a parachute and even a tank.

The early 19th century

THE skills of painters continued to develop after the age of Rubens (1577–1640). Some artists perfected their technique for imitating the real world in the finest detail. Others, such the great Dutch painter Rembrandt van Rijn (1606–69), showed how artists could also convey mood, atmosphere and personal feeling in their work. These two tendencies – technical clarity and artistic expression – remained the central themes in the changing styles of art during the early 19th century.

◪ PARIS SALON

By the 19th century, the focus of European art had switched from Italy to France. Each year, the public crowded into the exhibition of the French Royal Academy of Painting and Sculpture, called the Salon, to see the latest works, as shown in this painting by François Biard (1798–1882).

◧ JACQUES-LOUIS DAVID

One of the leading French painters in about 1800 was Jacques-Louis David (1748–1825). He tried to recreate the glory of ancient Roman and Greek times with a grand style called Neoclassicism. This heroic mood is seen in his portrait of the French leader, *Napoleon Crossing the Alps* (1800).

◪ GUSTAVE COURBET

Until the 1850s, only a limited range of subjects was thought to be 'noble' enough for fine art – history, Greek, and Roman mythology, landscapes and flattering portraits. The French painter Gustave Courbet (1819–77) reacted against this by painting ordinary, working people and the hardships of their daily lives, as seen in *The Corn-Sifters* (1865). He called this new approach 'Realism'.

ART AND BEAUTY

The English painter Edward Burne-Jones (1833–98) took a very different view of art to Courbet's Realism. He wrote: 'I mean by a picture a beautiful romantic dream, of something that never was, never will be – in a light better than any that ever shone – in a land no one can define...'.

◪ FORMAL TRAINING

In France, artists were trained to paint in schools called academies. The teachers were often very gifted artists, who could paint with technical brilliance. But the strict teaching rules of these schools tended to stifle personal flair, and artists who trained in them often produced technically correct, but dull work.

▣ THÉODORE GÉRICAULT

During the decades around 1800, a movement called Romanticism influenced both paintings and writing. It championed feelings – emotion, love, despair, the sublime. One of the most famous paintings of the time was *The Raft of the Medusa* (1819), by French artist Théodore Géricault (1791–1824), which depicts the ordeal of the survivors of a real-life shipwreck.

▢ PRE-RAPHAELITES

In 1848 a group of English artists began a movement called the Pre-Raphaelite Brotherhood, hoping to re-create the simplicity of early Italian art before the time of Raphael (1483–1520). They painted romantic pictures of great technical brilliance, often of scenes from the Bible, or from mythology or medieval history. *The Mirror of Venus* is by the English painter Edward Burne-Jones.

The late 19th century

DURING the 1870s, a new, energetic art movement developed in France. A group of painters, including Claude Monet (1840–1926), Pierre-Auguste Renoir (1841–1919), Camille Pissarro (1830–1903), and Alfred Sisley (1839–99), set out to paint the world around them. To capture a sense of immediacy, they painted outdoors and quickly, using rapid brushstrokes. Their movement was called 'Impressionism'. It changed forever the way that European artists approached painting.

◄ RENOIR

A painting such as *The Swing* (1876), by Renoir, shows how the Impressionists built up their pictures using dabs of colour, rather than strong shapes and lines. They shared a desire to capture on canvas the visual effects of dappled sunlight, and used blue instead of black for shadows.

◥ SYMBOLISM

In contrast to the Impressionists, who painted the world they saw around them, many later artists wanted to paint the world of the imagination. Works by artists such as the French painter Paul Sérusier (1864–1927) evoked the mood of dreams, myths and poetry.

◻ VAN GOGH

The Dutch painter Vincent van Gogh (1853–90) adopted the Impressionist style of painting. But he also conveyed a new sense of intense feeling in his work, seen in the vigorous dabs and swirls of paint in *Siesta* (1889–90). Because he took Impressionism one step further, Van Gogh is known as a 'Post-Impressionist' (*post* meaning 'after' in Latin).

☑ MONET

The Impressionists exhibited together for the last time in 1886, after which other styles of art took over. But Claude Monet lived on for another 40 years, always experimenting with the Impressionist style, and creating vibrant fields of colour, as in his waterlily series of paintings.

◪ POINTILLISM

The French artist Georges Seurat (1859–91) took the Impressionist technique to its logical conclusion. Instead of using dabs of paint, he created paintings made up entirely of tiny dots of colour, as seen in his *Circus Parade* (1887–88). This style is known as Pointillism.

☑ BRUSHWORK

Impressionist artists broke away from the European tradition of realistic, detailed work, and felt free to apply paint in any way they chose. Vigorous brushstrokes, as in this harbour scene by the Spanish painter Joaquin Sorolla y Bastida (1863–1923) gave their work a vibrant sense of movement.

NOT APPRECIATED

Van Gogh's works, such as his sunflower paintings, are now worth millions. But in his lifetime they were not appreciated at all. Mentally disturbed, he committed suicide in 1890, having sold just one painting.

The 20th century

IN THE early 1900s, young artists began to explore new ways of painting. They stopped trying to imitate the real world, which had been the main aim of art since the Renaissance, and instead experimented with bright, unrealistic colours and shapes, rearranging the spaces that we see in the real world. The Cubists explored ways of showing how something might look if it was broken down into geometric shapes, such as cubes, and viewed from several different angles at once. Other artists made 'abstract art' by arranging shapes and colours.

◪ **PICASSO**
The Spanish artist Pablo Picasso (1881–1973) was one of the leaders of the Cubist movement, which lasted from 1907 to about 1914. He is celebrated as perhaps the greatest artist of the 20th century.

◪ **CUBISM**
One of the three main Cubist painters was the Spaniard Juan Gris (1887–1927), whose *Landscape, Ceret* (1913) is shown here. Cubism challenged the traditional use of perspective, which allowed three-dimensional space to be shown on a flat surface. Instead, the subject of the painting was broken up into shapes, which were then rearranged.

◪ **JACKSON POLLOCK**
In the second half of the 20th century, the focus of modern art shifted from Europe to the United States. A leading figure was Jackson Pollock (1912–56). He created large, abstract pictures by splashing paint onto a canvas on the floor – a style known as Abstract Expressionism.

SURREALISM

During the 1920s, a group of artists set out to paint images of the unconscious mind, creating bizarre, dreamlike pictures, often in lifelike detail. One of these 'surrealists' was the Belgian painter René Magritte (1898–1967), who also enjoyed playing with words. His picture of a pipe was labelled 'This is not a pipe'.

◰ DALI

The Spanish painter Salvador Dali (1904–89) is famous for his strange, dreamlike paintings with oddly extended bodies, melting watches and half-open drawers set in desert landscapes, all painted in meticulous detail. He became the best known of the surrealists, partly because his real life was almost as bizarre as his paintings.

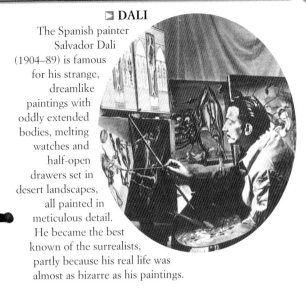

◲ EXPRESSIONISM

The style of painting known as Expressionism began in Germany and France in about 1905. Painters expressed emotions with strong colours, vigorous brushstrokes, and distorted images. *The Harvest* (1928) is by Constant Permeke (1885–1952), a leading Belgian Expressionist.

◱ COLLAGE

The word 'collage' comes from the French *coller* – 'to stick'. In their efforts to break away from traditional ways of painting, the Cubists began to stick printed words, music, and bits of wallpaper into their works. The Surrealists, such as the German Max Ernst (1891–1976), took this a step further, and created whole pictures out of images cut from printed books and magazines.

Techniques of painting

THE changing styles of painting over the centuries have often reflected the kinds of materials that were available to artists. For instance, the Impressionists were able to paint landscapes in the open air because, after 1841, oil paint was sold in small, easily portable tubes. Each kind of paint – oil paint, watercolour or modern water-based acrylic – behaves in a different way, and produces its own distinctive effects.

◥ FRESCO

To create murals that would last for decades or even centuries, medieval artists in Italy, such as Giotto, applied water-based paint to plaster that was still wet, or fresh. The technique was called fresco (from the Italian for fresh). Painters had to colour small patches of plaster before it dried.

◥ OIL PAINT

With oil paint, the colour, or 'pigment', is mixed with an oil such as clove or linseed oil. The paint can be applied very thickly, so the brushstrokes still show. Vincent van Gogh used this technique, known as 'impasto', in the painting shown here. Thick oil paint may take many weeks to dry fully.

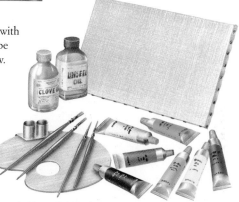

◢ ARTISTS' MATERIALS

Artists using oil paints work on a canvas, which is stretched over a wooden frame and propped on an easel. Using an animal-hair brush, they mix the colours on their palette, perhaps adding turpentine to make it thinner.

❏ WATER COLOUR

With watercolour, the pigment is mixed with water and then applied to paper. Watercolour paints are easy to carry around, and they dry quickly. But it is hard to correct mistakes. One of the greatest watercolourists was the English painter John Sell Cotman (1782–1842), who painted *The Ruins of Rievaulx Abbey* in 1803.

✓ COLOUR WHEEL

The three primary colours are red, yellow, and blue. These can be mixed together to form orange, green and purple. On a colour wheel, one primary colour will appear opposite the mixture of the two other primary colours (for example, red will appear opposite green, which is a mixture of yellow and blue). These opposites are called complementary colours.

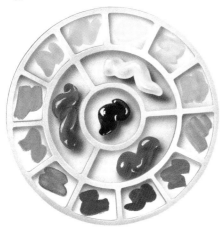

✓ MIXING COLOURS

Modern paints are manufactured in many shades, based on mixtures of the primary colours, as well as black and white. They have special names such as burnt umber, cadmium yellow, cobalt blue and phthalo green. These can be mixed together to produce just about any colour found in nature. As a rule, artists mix colours on their palette before applying them to the painting.

PIGMENTS

In the past, the colour (or pigment) used in paints was based on naturally occurring substances, such as extracts of plants. Today, many pigments are made using synthetic chemical dyes, such as the phthalocyanine used to make phthalo green (shown here).

Printed art

MOST paintings are made as individual pieces of work. This gives them extra value, but generally means few people see the work. The advantage of printing is that an image can be reproduced many times. People have known how to print since ancient times. By cutting an image into a flat surface – such as a block of wood or stone, or even a slice of potato – and then smearing it with ink, the image can be transferred to paper many times over. In Europe, printing has been used to mass-produce art since the 15th century.

◁ WOODBLOCKS

The Japanese became very skilled at making woodblock prints. In the 19th century, Ando Hiroshige (1797–1858) produced a series of famous landscapes. Each colour was applied separately, using as many as 20 blocks to make each print.

◹ ANDY WARHOL

One of the most famous modern artists to use printing was the American Andy Warhol (1928–87). In his 'Pop Art', he chose as his subjects mass-market images such as soup cans, and printed multiple copies of them using the silkscreen process.

Der Musik Unterricht

◹ ENGRAVING

This early 19th-century print was made in Austria using a method called engraving. To make an engraving, lines were cut into a metal plate with a sharp tool called a burin. Ink was then rubbed into the lines, so they could be printed onto paper. Colours were usually painted in later by hand.

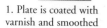
1. Plate is coated with varnish and smoothed

2. An image is scratched into the varnish

3. Plate is immersed in an acid bath

4. Varnish is removed

LITHOGRAPHY

In the method of printing called lithography (after the Greek *lithos*, 'stone'), originally the image was drawn onto stone with a wax crayon, then the stone was covered in water. When oily printer's ink was applied, it ran off the water, but stuck to the wax, so the image could be transferred to paper. Modern colour printing uses metal sheets, but the same principles apply.

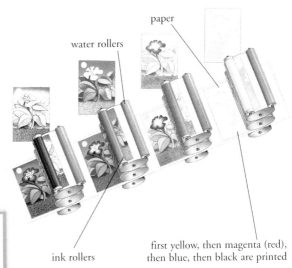

paper

water rollers

ink rollers

first yellow, then magenta (red), then blue, then black are printed

TOULOUSE-LAUTREC

Lithography was invented in 1798, and artists were quick to see its advantages. It allowed them to draw freely, in a way that was not possible with other printing methods. The French painter Henri de Toulouse-Lautrec (1841–1901) used lithography to produce his famous posters, such as this one advertising a new novel (1892).

SILKSCREEN

In silkscreen printing, a stencil image is cut out of paper and stuck to a fine-mesh screen that has been stretched over a frame. The screen is laid over a blank sheet of paper, and ink is pushed across the screen using a rubber blade. This ensures that the image is transferred evenly to the paper.

ETCHING

Etching is an old printing method in which acid is used to 'etch', or bite into, metal. First, a copper plate is covered in a kind of acid-resistant varnish. The artist creates an image by scratching through the varnish to the metal. The plate is covered with acid, which cuts into the metal only where the artist has drawn. Then the plate is cleaned and rubbed with ink, so the lines can be printed onto paper.

5. Ink is pressed onto plate

6. Excess ink is wiped away

7. Paper is laid over plate and pressed with a roller

Stone sculpture

SCULPTURE may be an even older form of art than painting. Small limestone sculptures, such as the Venus of Willendorf, found in Austria, date back to 25,000 BC. Stone is hard to carve, but sculptures made from it have one great advantage – they last just about forever. Long after virtually all other remains of a civilization have rotted away, the stone sculptures survive. This is why stone sculpture has played such an important part in the history of art and civilization.

◩ GREEK SCULPTURE

The ancient Greeks were the greatest sculptors of the ancient world. They used sculpture to decorate their temples. This head of Medusa was found at the Temple of Apollo at Didyma, Turkey. The Greeks were also expert at turning stone – usually the fine stone called marble – into lifelike imitations of real people.

◩ EGYPTIAN GODS

The ancient Egyptians developed their own style of religious sculpture, which followed sacred rules. It was usually rather stiff and formal, like this pair of gods, Seth and Nephthys, sculpted during the time of Ramses II, who reigned about 1292–25 BC.

◩ ROMAN SCULPTURE

The Romans followed the Greek approach to sculpture, and many Greek sculptors went to work in Rome. The very realistic, life-size marble sculpture of *The Dying Gaul* is a Roman copy of a Greek bronze statue made about 220 BC.

MODERN SCULPTURE

Not all ancient cultures tried to imitate real life in their art. This was the case with the sculpture of ancient Mexico. Modern sculptors likewise have taken a much freer and more imaginative approach to their work, not only in Mexico – where this work comes from – but all over the world. They shifted away from the idea of imposing a specific meaning on the stone, to one of working with the material, letting it guide them. Abstract sculpture did not become common until the 1950s.

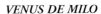

MICHELANGELO

Inspired by Roman sculpture that was found during the Renaissance, the Italian artist Michelangelo Buonarroti (1475–1564) became the greatest sculptor in stone since ancient times. He could turn blocks of marble into extraordinarily life-like and tender works. His figure of *Moses* was created for the tomb of Pope Julius II (c.1513–45).

CLAY SCULPTURE

Baked clay can last almost as long as stone, although it is more easily broken. This clay model of a potter comes from the Bahia culture of Ecuador, and is at least 1500 years old. There is an important difference between clay sculpture and stone sculpture, however. Stone sculpture is created by chipping away from a block of stone, whereas clay sculpture is made by manipulating – or 'modelling' – the clay while it is still soft.

VENUS DE MILO

One of the most famous pieces of ancient Greek sculpture, carved in about 150 BC, now stands in the Louvre in Paris. It was found on a beach on the Greek island of Milos in 1820. It is thought to represent the Greek ideal of female beauty.

Bronze sculpture

AN ANCIENT method of making long-lasting sculpture was to cast it in metal. First of all the sculptor has to make the original model, usually out of a soft material that is easy to carve, such as clay, plaster or wax. Then a mould is made, usually by wrapping the model in clay. Lastly, molten metal is poured into the mould, so it takes the shape of the original model. Methods like these have been used to cast sculpture in gold and copper, but the usual metal used for sculpture is bronze, which is a mixture of copper and tin.

INCA GOLD
The Inca civilization, which flourished in the Andes Mountains of South America more than 500 years ago, made jewellery, tools and delicate sculptures from gold, such as this small religious figure. To do this, they often used the 'lost wax method'. First, a model was made from beeswax. This was covered in clay, which made a mould. When the mould was heated, the wax melted and drained away. It was replaced with molten gold.

PLASTER MODEL
One of the greatest sculptors of the late 19th century was Auguste Rodin (1840–1917) of France. He was famous for his very lifelike statues, made in stone or bronze. His biggest project was *The Gates of Hell*, for a Paris museum. He never finished it, but after his death several bronze casts were made from his plaster model.

EARLY BRONZES
One advantage of bronze over marble is that bronze can carry heavy weights on thin supports. Bronze was ideal, therefore, for making sculptures of horses and their riders, such as this first-century-BC statuette of a horseman from Turkey.

◧ BRONZE CASTING

In ancient times, bronze was used to make weapons and tools. First, rocks containing copper and tin ores were mined from underground. These were heated until the metals melted and could be separated from the rocks. Ingots of copper and tin were then heated together to make bronze. The molten bronze was poured into a mould. 'Casting' the bronze into an object was a highly skilled job.

copper and tin ores are heated together

bronze sword

molten bronze is poured into mould

◧ SCULPTURE AND ARCHITECTURE

Modern engineering techniques have allowed artists to create sculpture on a huge scale. The *Atomium*, shown here, was built for the international fair held in Brussels in 1958. Its nine huge steel balls, rising to 396 feet (120 meters), represent a giant model of an atom.

◧ HENRY MOORE

Henry Moore (1898–1986) was Britain's leading 20th-century sculptor. His work was usually based on the human form, as in his bronze *King and Queen* (1952–53). But sometimes his figures were less easily recognized, and appear as rounded shapes pierced with holes.

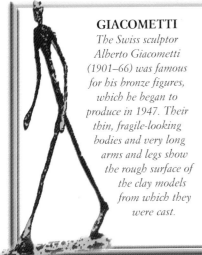

GIACOMETTI

The Swiss sculptor Alberto Giacometti (1901–66) was famous for his bronze figures, which he began to produce in 1947. Their thin, fragile-looking bodies and very long arms and legs show the rough surface of the clay models from which they were cast.

Photography

THE oldest surviving photograph was taken in 1827. Cameras and photographic techniques developed rapidly in the decades that followed. By the 1860s, it was possible to take very good portraits and landscape pictures in black and white, and some photographers were beginning to see photography as an art form. This was one reason why the Impressionists and later artists decided that they had to do more with painting than simply copy reality, which photography could do better.

hole collects image of the outside world and mirror projects it into the room

dark room

light table

projected image on light table

◩ CAMERA OBSCURA

The word 'camera' comes from an old invention called a camera obscura (Latin for 'dark room') – a room in which a 'live' picture of the outside world is projected onto a dish through a small hole in the roof. The breakthrough of photography was the discovery of a way to capture this picture permanently, using light-sensitive chemicals.

◪ PHOTOGRAPHY AND ART

Photography came to influence many painters. The French artist Edgar Degas (1834–1917) tried to imitate the more spontaneous, unposed compositions often seen in photographs.

◩ CARTE DE VISITE

Photography enabled people to have affordable pictures of themselves for the first time. During the 1860s, hundreds of photographic studios were set up around the world to take portrait photographs the size of a visiting card, or *carte de visite*. Millions of portraits were taken – a craze that was known as 'cartomania'.

HENRI CARTIER-BRESSON

The French photographer Henri Cartier-Bresson (b.1908) is celebrated for his numerous unusual compositions of 20th-century people and events. Many of his pictures contain a number of points of interest – rather like this photo of him in New York, holding his famous Leica camera.

DAGUERREOTYPE

The pioneers of early photography experimented with various methods. The daguerreotype was invented by Frenchman Louis Daguerre (1789–1851) in 1839. It produced excellent photographs on silver-coated copper sheets, but as there were no negatives, it was hard to make copies.

FASHION PHOTOGRAPHY

Photography has been used in magazines and for advertising since the 1880s. During the 20th century, many of the most famous photographers, such as the American Richard Avedon (b.1923), worked for fashion magazines like *Vogue*. In this 1960s edition, held by dress designer Mary Quant, the cover girl is the famous model Twiggy.

WAR PHOTOGRAPHY

Photographs have helped to show the grim, unglamorous side of war since 1855, when British photographer Roger Fenton took pictures of the Crimean War. Famous war photographers include the American Robert Capa (1913–54), who captured dramatic images of the Spanish Civil War and World War II.

Applied art

THE kind of paintings and sculpture found in museums and galleries is often referred to as 'fine art'. But a great deal of artistic creativity is also devoted to making ordinary or practical objects more beautiful – through what is known as 'applied art'. Fountains, for example, have a practical function, and yet they may spout from magnificent and elaborate works of sculpture. By and large, artists either make fine art or applied art, but some do both.

◨ SALT CELLAR

Benvenuto Cellini (1500–71) was a brilliant goldsmith and sculptor, and also one of the most wild and colourful characters of the Italian Renaissance. He created this magnificent piece for the king of France – as something to hold the salt on the dining table!

◨ PORCELAIN FIGURE

Great skills in both sculpture and painting have been applied to pottery figurines, created to decorate the living rooms of collectors. This Kakiemon porcelain figure of a man was made in Japan during the Edo period (1615–1867).

◨ TAPESTRY

Woollen wall hangings, or tapestries, had a practical purpose – they helped to keep rooms warm in the days before central heating. From medieval times on, expensive European tapestries were designed to look like paintings, often by great artists such as Rubens, and were woven by skilled craftworkers. These huge 17th-century tapestries are in the Château of Fontainebleau in France.

JEWELLERY

Careful design and fine craftsmanship have been applied to jewellery since ancient times. Beauty is, after all, a key feature of jewellery. In about 1900, the fashionable style called Art Nouveau brought a fresh, swirling elegance to jewellery design, as seen in this belt buckle and hair comb.

WALLPAPER

During the 19th century, improved manufacturing techniques made it possible to produce cheaper wallpaper. Good wallpaper patterns have a sense of balance and graceful elegance, like those produced by the English designer William Morris (1834–96), who based his designs on shapes drawn from nature. His work influenced many other designers, such as C.F.A. Voysey (1857–1941), who designed this wallpaper in 1909.

MURALS

Long before wallpaper was invented, walls were decorated with murals. The Etruscans, who lived in Italy before the Roman period, painted their tombs with delightful scenes of their lives and pleasures. Their homes may have been similarly decorated, but only the tombs have survived.

ISLAMIC TILEWORK

Muslim designers became very skilled at making patterns, particularly with glazed tiles. Generally, these were used on the inside walls and floors of buildings, but in Isfahan, in Iran, tiles also cover the domes of the mosques. This is the Royal Mosque of Abbas I, built from about 1590 to 1629. The bright blue colour of some of the tiles is also typical of the pottery of the region.

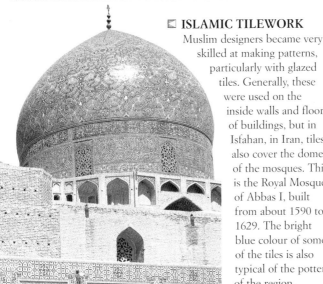

Commercial art

MOST artists find it hard to earn a living by selling paintings or sculpture. Many gifted painters instead use their skills to create the illustrations needed in the world of business – for example, advertising, packaging, CD covers, illustrated storybooks, magazine articles and instruction manuals. Illustrators are generally not able to choose what they draw or paint, but instead must follow instructions from the person who is buying their 'artwork'. They are briefed to create images for a specific task.

◪ COMIC STRIPS

Stories told in pictures have existed since ancient times. The hilarious storybook *Struwelpeter* (from which this illustration is taken) was written by the German writer Heinrich Hoffmann in 1845. It was a forerunner of the first comics for children, which appeared in the 1890s.

◪ FAIRY TALES

Illustrations for children's books became ever more elaborate as the techniques of colour printing improved. The gifted British illustrator, painter and caricaturist Richard Doyle (1824–83) produced this picture for a book called *Adventures in Fairyland*.

◪ ADVERTISING

Art has played a role in advertising since the early days of printing in the 1500s. Businesses soon realized that mass-produced posters could attract more public attention if they included a striking picture, as on this 1930s advertisement for tea.

BUY INDIAN TEA

☑ POSTERS

Some of the most famous posters in the history of advertising were produced in Paris in the late 19th century, at the time when Toulouse-Lautrec was making his lithographs. An 1898 poster for the celebrated nightspot the Folies Bergère, by Paul Berthon (1848–1909), is typical of the era.

◪ MAGAZINES

Hundreds of illustrated magazines were launched in the 19th century, benefiting from cheaper printing and a wide distribution by trains. This edition of the illustrated weekly *Jugend* ('Youth') was published in Germany in 1897.

▣ LOGO

Artistic design is applied to company 'logos', such as the VW badge that appears on Volkswagen cars. The best logos are simple, but instantly recognizable – and are much harder to design than most people imagine.

COMPUTER ART

The computer is a powerful new tool for artists. Because of their huge memories, computers can generate and alter a vast range of images, at great speed.

A R T

The art world

A GREAT many people are involved in the world of art, including those who buy and sell paintings and sculpture, those who work in galleries, and the art directors who commission illustrations for magazines and other publications. But the most important people of all are the artists who create the paintings, sculpture, and other works of art. In the technical and commercial age of the 21st century, the world needs their creative talent as much as it has ever done.

◢ NORMAN ROCKWELL
The work of commercial artists is generally not valued as highly as the work of the great masters. One exception was the American painter Norman Rockwell (1894–1978). He was famous for his images of American life, painted for the cover of *The Saturday Evening Post*.

◀ THE ARTIST'S STUDIO
Most artists paint in a special room called a studio. In the past, the most famous artists had big studios, like that of Rubens, shown here. They employed numerous assistants to help them.

◤ THE LOUVRE
The Louvre in Paris contains one of the world's greatest collections of European art. Once a royal palace, it was extended in the 17th century to house the growing royal collection, which the public was allowed to visit after 1681. In 1989 it was given a new, ultramodern entrance under a glass pyramid.

AUCTIONS

Many works of art by the old masters are owned by private collectors. If they want to sell one, they usually go to a leading auction house, where, on an advertised date, the work is sold to the highest bidder.

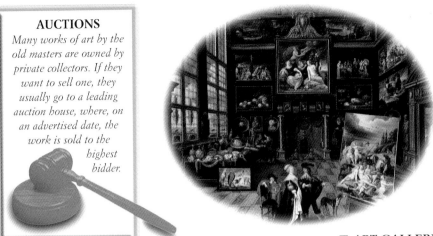

◪ ART GALLERIES

Originally, galleries were places where private collectors of art kept their paintings and sculpture. Art dealers also had galleries, where collectors could view works of art that were for sale. The pictures often covered the walls, as in this 17th-century painting. The first public galleries were opened in the 1600s.

◪ ROYAL COLLECTIONS

Fine art is considered to be a symbol of wealth, culture and good taste. The Queen of England has inherited a large and very valuable collection, including works by Leonardo da Vinci, Michelangelo, Holbein, Rubens, and many others. They can be seen at Buckingham Palace (shown here) and Windsor Castle.

◪ STREET ART

Some artists do not make art that can be collected. Street artists draw in chalk on the pavements, and collect small gifts of money from admiring passers-by. At the end of the day, the picture is erased or washed away by the rain.

History of Culture

THE word 'culture' is often used to describe art forms that are enjoyed by only a few people – such as opera or ballet. But 'culture' can mean much more than that. It can describe someone's upbringing and education, their religious faith, their community's traditions, and their nation's language, literature and art. It can also describe how a person lives, their political ideas, and how they identify themselves. Usually, 'culture' refers to all these things together, and is used to describe a unique civilization of a particular time or people.

What does culture do?

WITHIN each society or civilization, culture has many separate functions. Books, films, plays and music can simply amuse and entertain, or they can be challenging and thought provoking. They can reinforce traditional values, or inspire people with unsettling new ideas. Practicing ancient forms of culture – from craftwork to folk dancing – can be a way of preserving a treasured heritage, or maintaining a threatened way of life. During the 20th century, mass culture became a valuable commodity, sold by global corporations to consumers in many lands.

ANCIENT CULTURE

The Roma people – sometimes known as 'Gypsies'– have preserved their ancient nomadic way of life for hundreds of years, along with their own language, customs, crafts and musical traditions. Originally from northern India, Roma now live in many parts of Europe and northern Africa.

SEGREGATION

Ideas about culture often play an important part in politics. In South Africa, from the 1950s to the 1990s the white rulers forced black and white people to be kept apart, or segregated, claiming that white culture was 'better' than the local African civilization.

MASS MEDIA

During the 20th century, mass media – films, TV, and magazines – were able to reach a worldwide audience. Children were no longer entertained just by local or regional stories. Although films made in the West, such as *The Lion King,* are hugely popular, they can also weaken local cultures.

◪ FOLK FESTIVAL

Around 1800, the Industrial Revolution changed the way people lived. Many skills and crafts died out. But people like these Breton folk dancers from France keep alive their culture by celebrating it in folk festivals.

◪ TRADITIONAL LIFESTYLE

For many peoples, following their traditional lifestyle is a way of keeping their culture alive. In northwest Canada, for example, some Inuit men still hunt seals for their skins, meat and blubber, waiting for the seals to surface at ice holes.

◪ HIGH CULTURE

Opera stars such as Russian singer Galina Vishnevskaya spend many years training to reach international standards. Only the best succeed. Opera music is often described as 'high culture' – because it can be difficult to understand, and is not popular with everyone.

NATIONAL PRIDE

On July 4, Americans celebrate their independence from British rule by having a national Independence Day holiday. The national flag – 'The Star-Spangled Banner' – is flown proudly everywhere.

Belonging

FOR most people, a sense of belonging is very important. People like – and need – to feel that they are not alone. Most people feel love or loyalty towards a small group, such as their family. Some are loyal to large organizations, such as the company they work for, or their school. Many people also feel deeply attached to the place where they live, or to the country where they were born. Belonging to a political party can be important, too. And increasingly, young people show loyalty to designer logos or well-known brands. All these feelings of belonging help define, or shape, the culture of individuals and whole communities.

◢ **THE 'BIG M'**
Many international corporations, such as McDonald's, use a logo on all their buildings and products. The logo attracts customers anywhere in the world. When people see it they feel safe, because they know exactly what products the company sells.

◣ **HOLY SIGN**
The cross on the roof of this simple white building in Greece tells passers-by that it is a Christian church. For Christians, the cross is a holy sign. It reminds them of the wooden frame on which Jesus Christ was executed in about AD 30. People from other faiths also use holy signs. Muslims use a crescent moon to symbolize Islam, and Jewish people use a six-pointed Star of David.

◣ **RITUAL OF SHARING**
In many Christian churches, the most important religious ceremony involves sharing holy bread and wine. Worshippers take part in this ritual – called the Mass, Holy Communion or Eucharist – to feel closer to God and to their fellow Christians. The ritual recalls Christ's Last Supper with his disciples.

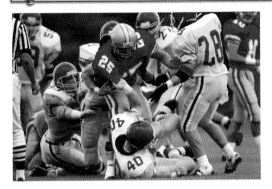

◪ TEAM COLOURS

Members of national or local sports teams all wear the same style of clothing, in the same colours. This helps them identify other team members on the field, when play is fast and furious. Wearing identical clothes also helps build team spirit – the players are united not just in appearance, but also in their loyalty to each other and their desire to beat the opposition.

◪ WEDDING RINGS

Married couples in many countries wear wedding rings to show their lifelong commitment to one another. The custom of wearing a wedding ring on the fourth finger of the left hand originated in Europe, probably over 2000 years ago. People believed that a vein from this finger led to the heart.

FLAGS

Flags originated as banners, carried to help soldiers follow their leaders into battle. Now they are important national symbols, carried in processions at international events and flown on public holidays. These are the flags of Asia.

◪ IN UNIFORM

Dressed in uniform, these US guards of honour are lined up on parade for inspection. For all armed forces and public services, such as the police, uniforms are a sign of belonging. Officers demand very high standards of neatness as a way of encouraging self-respect and discipline.

Words and music

THROUGHOUT history, different cultures have expressed their values, beliefs and ideas in poems, songs and stories. Through the spoken or written word, a culture's beliefs were communicated to the wider world. In the past, different traditions in words and music identified groups within each society – and sometimes caused quarrels between peoples or nations. Today, people can enjoy an amazing variety of styles – some modern, others from long ago, or from far-distant countries with very different cultures.

◪ CHURCH CHRONICLE
Some of the earliest history writers were medieval monks. They wrote brief comments about important events in the margins of official church calendars. Their comments were collected together as 'chronicles'.

◪ MESSENGER
The Incas of South America (c. AD 1100 to 1530) ruled a huge empire. Unable to read or write, they used relay runners, called *chasquis*, to memorize and carry messages across the Andes Mountains.

◪ FIRESIDE TALE
During the 19th century, families gathered round the fire to listen to stories told by grandfather. Passing on stories and anecdotes from one generation to the next was a way of keeping a culture's beliefs and values alive. Many stories contained a message that taught young people how to behave.

◻ MINSTREL

Medieval minstrels played to entertain lords and ladies in their castles. They often composed their own songs and poems, praising brave heroes or beautiful women. Minstrels were especially famous for writing songs about romantic love. For hundreds of years after their music was forgotten, their ideas remained popular in Europe.

NOBLE POETESS

In many civilizations, learning how to write poetry was part of every nobleman's education. A few noblewomen learned, too, including Sei Shonagon, who lived at the royal court in Japan (c. 966 to 1017).

◻ EPIC NOVELS

From about AD 1700, writers in Europe began to create long, epic novels. Love was a classic theme, but it was treated very differently by authors from different countries, who brought to their works a flavor of their own culture's social manners. *Doctor Zhivago*, by Russian author Boris Pasternak (1890–1960), combines passion with political drama.

◻ GOOD VERSUS EVIL

All around the world, traditional stories describe battles between the forces of good and evil. Often, these tales have a religious or political meaning, and are hundreds of years old. During the 20th century, American movie makers used the theme of good versus evil to create some of their most successful stories. Westerns, gangster films, spy movies, and space adventures, such as *Star Wars*, all feature fights between characters representing good and evil.

Houses and homes

TODAY, just as in the past, people's houses are shaped by many different factors, such as their wealth, rank and the size of their family. The design and construction of people's homes is also influenced by the climate, by local building techniques, and by what materials are available. The layout of a house is often closely linked to a culture's ideas about the right way to live. In countries where women are not expected to work outside the home. For example, some houses are built with separate female quarters, and craftworkers' homes may include a workshop.

◩ THATCHED ROOF

Many traditional building styles are hundreds of years old. This stone-walled, straw-thatched house in Peru is built to a design used by the Incas, who ruled the Andes over 500 years ago. Like Inca houses, it has a walled courtyard.

◩ ROCK HOUSE

Some of the earliest human houses, made over 50,000 years ago, were simple shelters built in the mouths of caves or under overhanging rocks. This house in Portugal is based on the same ancient idea. It uses a natural feature in the landscape to provide a person with rugged protection from the wind and rain.

◳ PAPER WALLS

In Japan, traditional houses were designed to withstand frequent earthquakes. Their walls were made of paper stretched over bamboo poles. If an earthquake was slight, the walls would tremble but stay up. If it was severe, they would collapse without killing the people inside.

▣ IRON AND GLASS

Tall 'skyscraper' office and apartment buildings tower over a lake in Vancouver, Canada. The first skyscraper, which was made using a strong metal frame, was designed in 1885. Now, skyscrapers dominate the skyline of most modern cities, and range from poor housing to stylish offices.

▣ LOG CABIN

In regions with plentiful timber, such as Canada, Russia, and northern Europe, many traditional homes are built of wood – a cheaper material than imported brick or stone.

MOVABLE HOME

Nomadic peoples, like the Mongols of Central Asia, live in homes that are easy to move. The Mongols take their 'yurts' – domed tents made of thick felt – with them when they go in search of new grazing land for their flocks.

▣ STATELY HOME

Some of the world's most splendid houses were built for nobility and royalty, by the most skilled builders and craftworkers. This grand house with its elegant garden was designed for a noble family in Portugal, about 1670.

Food for all

FOOD plays an important part in the world's many different cultures. In some countries, such as Italy or India, it is immensely varied from one region to another. But universally, eating good food is enjoyed. In many cultures, sharing food with other people is considered a duty, and is a tradition that dates back thousands of years. As soon as early humans learned to grow crops, peasants spent their lives growing, cooking and preserving food to feed their families. Today, many people are still employed in farming and fishing, as well as in food-processing factories and supermarkets. But although people in richer countries can eat foods from anywhere in the world at any time of year, many people in poorer regions continue to face starvation.

◪ EATING TOGETHER

Sharing a meal, as this Japanese-American family is doing, is one of the oldest pleasures known. It is a way for family members to come together at the end of a busy day to share their news and enjoy their favourite food. For Asian people, it is a cultural tradition to eat food using two chopsticks held in one hand.

◪ RICE GROWING

In east Asia, rice has been grown in flooded paddies for thousands of years. In the past, local communities depended on food crops grown in the nearby fields. But today, many of the food crops grown by people in poor countries are sent to feed the people of rich nations.

◪ SUPERMARKET

The first supermarkets opened in about the 1950s. For the first time, people could help themselves to prepacked goods displayed on open shelves. Supermarkets claim to make shopping faster, easier, and more enjoyable. But some people today argue that they have too much control over the farmers who produce the food.

FOOD AID

Famines are often the result of natural disasters, or too much or too little rainfall. Emergency supplies from other countries are sent by truck to people in need.

▣ FOOD FOR FUN

In countries where the weather is dry and sunny for much of the year, outdoor cooking is very popular. Simple food, such as steaks or sausages, are grilled over charcoal on a 'barbecue'. The word means frame of sticks' and originated in the Caribbean.

▣ FAST FOOD

Burger and chips are a favourite 'fast food' – a meal that comes in a box and can be eaten at table or carried out. Prepared in huge quantities in factories, the food items are shipped for final cooking to 'outlets' all over the world. The cooking and serving procedures are strictly controlled. Although fast food is extremely popular, food experts fear that eating too much of it is unhealthy.

▣ OFF TO MARKET

In Africa and many other parts of the developing world, women grow food for their families on small garden plots. They carry any surplus produce, like these bananas – which will rot if not eaten quickly – to local markets to sell. This may mean a long journey, for little pay.

Looking good

HOW can a person tell which culture someone else belongs to? Mostly, they can find clues in the person's clothes, hairstyle, and makeup – all of which tell us something about who the other person is. Clothes may reflect someone's religion, ethnic origin, or even political views. A uniform provides information about skills, training, or rank. Traditional 'costumes' are often woven by hand from natural fibres, and may be decorated with local patterns. Fashion items are often made from artificial fibres and are produced in great quantities in factories. They may display popular designer labels.

NATIONAL DRESS

National costumes, like these from 19th-century Hungary, are a symbol of pride and are closely linked to the local culture. They reflect local weather, products (wool or silk), and ideas about decency.

OLD AND YOUNG

Old people and young children prefer to dress in their own styles. The elderly often choose formal clothes that follow a tradition, while children like to wear the latest fashions. Teenagers enjoy wearing clothes that rebel against formal traditions and shock older generations.

SPORT OUTFITS

Sport clothes, like the tops and pants worn by these gymnasts, are highly specialized. The fabric needs to bend and stretch with the body, fit closely, and be light, comfortable, and durable. The earliest sports clothes were made of natural fibres such as wool and cotton. Today, high-tech artificial fibres are used.

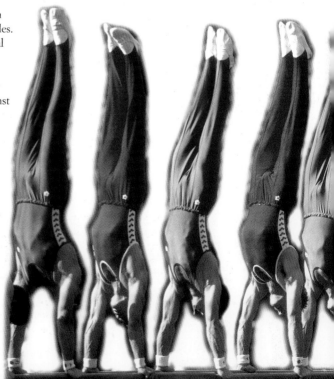

☑ FINISHING TOUCHES

A person who wears a neat hairstyle, makeup, and jewellery is indicating to others that he pr she cares about his or her appearance, and wants to look good. These adornments can indicate if they are rich or poor, married or single. This African girl has taken great care plaiting her many tiny braids, while her large metal earrings are a sign of wealth.

⬛ DRESSED FOR PRAYER

Many different faiths teach that men and women should be modestly dressed in public, and that they should wear special clothes when performing religious rituals, as a sign of respect. These Muslim women, who are on holy pilgrimage, have covered their heads and shoulders with a simple white garment. Jewish men also cover their heads and shoulders while reading from holy scriptures.

PROTEST CLOTHES

During the 1920s, young women 'flappers' cut their hair short, stopped wearing tight, uncomfortable corsets, and wore daringly short skirts as a way of demanding personal freedom and women's political rights.

☐ WESTERN STYLE

During the 20th century, many peoples all around the world stopped dressing in traditional costumes and began to wear Western-style clothes – as a way of showing that they had modern ideas. This Asian woman, for example, is wearing Western-style clothes while riding to work on her bicycle.

Life cycles

ALL around the world, people from different cultures have invented ceremonies to mark the important stages of a person's life. New babies are welcomed with naming rituals, or with ceremonies that enroll them in a particular religion. In many cultures, older children have to perform 'initiation' rituals, which are a way of proclaiming that they have reached adulthood. Marriage is often marked by rejoicing, and by an exchange of property between families. In many traditional cultures, the elderly are treated with respect. Almost everywhere, dead people are laid to rest with funeral prayers, which often express hope in a new life after death.

 **ROYAL BIRTH**
Most families share their pleasure at the birth of a new baby with their neighbours and friends. But rejoicing spreads to a wider public when the new baby is a royal prince or princess. This 16th-century painting from India shows people celebrating the birth of the Mongol prince Timur, who later ruled Samarkand in Central Asia.

INITIATION MASK
In many parts of the world, the change from childhood to adulthood is marked by special rituals. Groups of young men and women are taken away from their families to spend weeks with respected elders, who teach them local traditions and encourage them to develop skills they will need in adult life. Some take part in singing and dancing, and wear masks like this one from Africa.

GRAND MEMORIAL
Few people want to be forgotten after they are dead. Some are happy to be remembered by the people who have loved them. But others plan splendid monuments, like these temple-tombs in Madhya Pradesh, India. Powerful leaders and soldiers are often honoured by statues paid for by their governments.

HONOURED IN OLD AGE

In many traditional cultures, old people are honoured for the wisdom and experience they have gained during their lives. Younger people value what older men and women can teach them. In Asia, Confucius taught that it was a religious duty to respect old people while they were alive, and to make offerings to the spirits of dead ancestors. Very old people, like this dignified man, are regarded as 'national treasures' there.

SOLEMN FUNERAL

Priests, a choir, and members of a church congregation escort the coffin containing a dead friend to the graveside in this Polish funeral, held according to the traditions of the Roman Catholic Church. Many religious faiths teach that once a body has been laid to rest, the person's soul or spirit is freed to join God in Heaven or to be punished in Hell.

BIRTHDAYS

Birthdays are celebrated with parties and present-giving – a European and American cultural tradition. Cards are sent, too, and the birthday person is given a cake, decorated with lighted candles. Party guests usually sing the popular song 'Happy Birthday to You' (1935).

GETTING MARRIED

A Jewish bride and groom sip wine from a glass during their wedding ceremony, as a symbol of the joys and sorrows they will share together in the years ahead. In many cultures, marriage traditionally was considered to be a lifetime's commitment to one person. Most religions still teach this. But in many parts of Europe and the United States today, the tradition has changed – more than half of all marriages end in divorce.

Families

CHILDREN learn a great deal about the values and customs of their culture from other members of their families – particularly grandparents, who are often keen to pass on cultural traditions. Many civilizations place a high value on family life, seeing families as the best place to bring up children or to care for older people. Different cultures have their own ideas about the ideal size and structure of families. One kind is the 'nuclear' family – two parents and one or two children. Another kind is the 'extended' family, with several generations all living together.

◪ VICTORIAN VALUES

During the reign of Britain's Queen Victoria (1836–1901), families across Europe shared similar social ideals. It was a man's duty to work and provide for his family, while the woman cared for her husband, children and home.

◪ WORKING TOGETHER

During the 19th century, many families trekked westward across the United States and settled on the harsh prairies of the Midwest. They often lived a long way from their nearest neighbors, and had to be self-reliant and tough to survive. Men, women, and children all had their own 'chores' or tasks, to perform on the farm.

◪ UNREAL IDEAL?

In the United States during the 1950s, politicians and preachers urged all women to marry, have children and stay at home – even though many girls were well educated and wanted to have independent careers. The ideal of the happy family was promoted with pictures like this one, showing a clean, neat, well-dressed family with bright smiles.

◻ MANY GENERATIONS

Today, many families in Europe and North America consist of just two generations – parents and children. But traditionally, families were much larger, as they still are in many other parts of the world. This family from the island of Malta in the Mediterranean extends to four generations – grandparents to great-grandchildren. Often, aunts, uncles and cousins also share a family home.

◻ DESERT CLAN

For centuries, many families have relied on networks of close relatives, called 'clans' or 'tribes', to help them survive in harsh places such as the desert. Clan members, like these Bedouins from the deserts of Syria, owe loyalty to a chief and have a duty to help anyone belonging to the same tribe.

ONE CHILD ONLY

To prevent China from becoming overpopulated, the government passed a law forbidding parents to have more than one child. The law slowed the population growth, but sometimes led to problems with over-anxious parents and lonely children.

◻ WORKING MOTHER

In many countries single mothers are the head of the family. Some are widows and some have never married, but most are divorced. Many mothers – both single and married – work to support their children, and also find time to manage their homes. In some countries, companies provide childcare centres at the office.

Seasons of the year

IN THE past, the seasons played an important part in almost everyone's life. People depended on seasonal rains to water the crops – and if the rains failed, many died. Farmers prepared for the next season in advance, making sure they had the right seeds and tools ready for use. Religious leaders performed rituals asking their gods to send good weather at the most helpful times. And communities joined together to celebrate seasonal festivals such as May Day, Midwinter and harvest time. Today, people are protected from natural hazards by modern buildings, technology and medicines.

☑ MIDSUMMER GODDESS

Aine, the Irish goddess of love and fertility, was worshipped at Midsummer, when people lit bonfires on her hill. She was believed to be able to command the crops and animals.

◻ NEW YEAR FIREWORKS

In China, New Year is traditionally celebrated by setting off fireworks and firecrackers. The loud bangs are believed to frighten away evil spirits. Families decorate their doorways with streamers of red paper decorated with handwritten poems to bring good luck. Dancers carry huge paper lions and dragons, supported on sticks, through the streets. Clashing cymbals accompany the dancers. And to show their respect, children visit their teachers.

◻ SANTA CLAUS

In many parts of Europe and North America, young children believe that Santa Claus will bring them presents on Christmas Eve. 'Santa Claus' is a nickname for St. Nicholas, originally a bishop in Turkey. It was claimed he miraculously restored three young boys to life.

◻ RAIN DANCE

The weather is frequently unpredictable. For thousands of years, people have tried to influence local weather patterns by offering sacrifices to weather gods, saying prayers, or performing rituals. This Japanese rain dancer is wearing a broad-brimmed hat trimmed with a rainlike fringe. The dancer makes rapid movements and chants 'magic' words to encourage rain to fall.

SPRING BLOSSOMS

In Japan, families make special trips to the countryside to admire the first cherry blossoms of the year. Spring blooms have inspired many paintings and poems.

◻ FARMING YEAR

Until about 1800, most people lived in the country and relied on the crops they grew and the animals they raised for their survival. The seasons were of far greater significance to most people. Medieval manuscripts like this one show peasants performing a 'labour' or task for each month of the year. Here, the picture for April shows someone picking fruit in a rainshower, June shows a man plowing, in August the crops are being cut, and in December a pig is about to be killed for a winter feast.

◻ THANKSGIVING

Every year, on the fourth Thursday in November, American families celebrate Thanksgiving Day with a splendid meal. The first Thanksgiving was held in 1621 by settlers in Plymouth Colony, Massachusetts. They wanted to thank God for keeping them safe during the previous year, and for sending them a good harvest.

Celebrations

A CELEBRATION is a time when people get together to express joy at hearing some good news. People often celebrate an individual's achievement, such as exam success or the birth of a new baby. Some celebrations involve larger groups, or even whole nations. A political triumph, such as an election victory, may cause a whole country to cheer, while a religious festival such as Easter may be celebrated in towns and villages across the world. Many celebrations involve eating, giving presents and wearing special clothes. The normal rules of good behaviour are often relaxed as everyone shares in 'the festive spirit'.

◢ IMPERIAL CORONATION
From 1800 to 1812, Napoleon Bonaparte of France was the greatest general and most powerful ruler in Europe. He celebrated his success by holding a magnificent coronation ceremony for himself and his wife Josephine.

◩ EID UL-FITR
Muslims meet to pray at a mosque in Karachi, Pakistan, during the festival of Eid ul-Fitr – the Festival of Rejoicing. After prayers, many families hold parties for their friends and relatives, and make special gifts to charity. Eid ul-Fitr celebrates the end of the Islamic holy month of Ramadan, when Muslims fast from dawn to dusk to show devotion to Allah (God).

◤ THE END OF PROHIBITION
Between 1919 and 1933, the US government banned the manufacture and sale of all alcoholic drinks. It hoped to end drunkenness and improve public health. When Prohibition finally ended, huge parties were held to celebrate the news.

GRADUATION

Students who have successfully completed their studies at college take part in special graduation ceremonies. Each student is given a scroll listing their name and degree.

◤ TRIUMPHAL ARCH

The greatest reward that the Romans could give to an army general was a 'triumph' – a public celebration of his military victories. The general's procession marched through the streets and under a triumphal arch.

◧ DIWALI

Hindus and Sikhs celebrate Diwali – a festival of light – in October or November each year. Hindus say prayers to Lakshmi, the goddess of wealth. They decorate their homes with symbols of good fortune and light it with many candles.

◧ CARNIVAL

At carnivals, people dress in magnificent costumes and parade through the streets singing and dancing. This dancer is at the world-famous Rio Carnival in Brazil. Originally, Carnival was a Christian festival held at the beginning of Lent, a period of fasting in February or March – the word 'carnival' means 'farewell to meat'. People held special meals so that they could eat up all the meat that was forbidden in Lent.

Music and dance

BEFORE early humans learned to use language almost a million years ago, they used body movements and made grunts and squeals to communicate with each other. They also made music by tapping on shells, bones and wood, and by whistling. Today, simple sounds and body language still play an important part in music and dance. But over thousands of years, the world's many different cultures have developed their own distinctive styles of sound and movement to express their feelings. Many are easily recognizable, and are enjoyed by people all over the world.

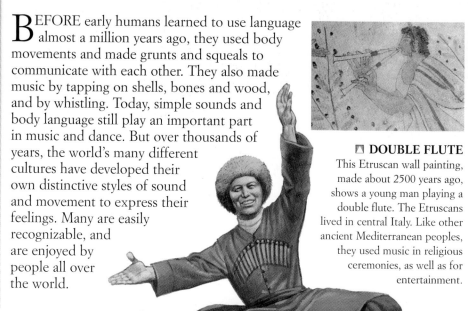

◪ **DOUBLE FLUTE**
This Etruscan wall painting, made about 2500 years ago, shows a young man playing a double flute. The Etruscans lived in central Italy. Like other ancient Mediterranean peoples, they used music in religious ceremonies, as well as for entertainment.

◧ **COSSACK DANCER**
A Cossack dancer from Ukraine leaps high in the air, showing off his agility. Cossacks were famous for their bravery and horse riding skills, and the men traditionally expressed their warlike energy in dramatic dances.

◧ **COUNTRY DANCE**
In many parts of northern Europe, people often enjoyed country dancing as a form of entertainment, particularly on long winter evenings. Dressed in traditional costume, this 19th-century Norwegian couple is dancing to the accompaniment of a fiddle, or violin. Traditional country dances feature elaborate patterns of steps. A popular dance for a larger group, or set, is the 'square dance', in which four couples face inward from four sides.

CHOIR OF NUNS

From about AD 500 to 1500, the most advanced – and probably the most beautiful – music in Europe was created for choirs of monks or nuns in church. They spent several hours each day chanting prayers and singing hymns. Because they were among the few people who could read and write, their music was written down in books. Many of these have survived, so ancient religious music can still be performed today.

FANCY FOOTWORK

During the 1920s, a new dance called the Charleston caused a sensation. Invented by African-Americans in Charleston, South Carolina, and danced to a jazzy rhythm, it featured fast, high-kicking, backward steps that made women's skirts fly high above the knees!

MUSIC FOR REBELS

Girl members of a Japanese punk rock band strike a defiant pose. For centuries, music has been a popular way of expressing protest against government power or social conventions – unwritten rules of good behaviour. Punk rock music originated in England in the 1970s, and was pioneered by bands such as the Sex Pistols. It was raw, energetic, violent and rebellious.

TEMPLE DANCER

Bharata-natyam is a dance tradition of the Tamil people of southern India. Almost 2000 years old, it originated among young women who served the gods and goddesses in temples. Seven dances are performed, beginning with a prayer and ending with a reading of ancient holy texts. A singer, drums and wind instruments accompany the dancer.

Performance

DRAMA – the portrayal on stage of human feelings and relationships – probably developed as a way of acting out myths and legends. Actors were able to bring the stories alive, conveying to an audience a range of emotions – anger, revenge, sorrow, love and happiness – which the audience could relate to their own lives. The ancient Greeks were the first people to build theatres. Their earliest plays were written for religious festivals – authors competed to have their tragedies or comedies performed. Gradually, over the centuries, different cultures around the world developed their own distinctive forms of drama.

◤ COMIC ACTOR
Roman comic actors, like the one depicted in this terracotta model, wore a slave's short tunic and a face mask with a menacing grin. Actors in large Greek and Roman theatres always wore masks, so that people in the back rows of seats could see their expressions. Different masks portrayed different characters – happy, fierce or sad.

◤ SHAKESPEARE'S GLOBE
William Shakespeare (1564–1616) is considered by most people to have written the greatest plays in the world. Many of them were written to be performed in the circular Globe playhouse in London. Men played all the parts, performing to a noisy audience of nobility and royalty, who sat in wooden bays, and servants, apprentices and other townsfolk who stood in front of the central stage.

◤ BEIJING OPERA
During the 18th and 19th centuries, lively, colourful operas were the most popular form of entertainment in China. They were often based on traditional stories or historical events, and featured acrobatic dancing, mock battles and comedy, as well as singing and orchestral music.

◨ EXPERIMENTAL STYLE

During the 20th century, theatre directors in many parts of Europe and the United States experimented with new styles of staging plays. They borrowed ideas from traditional theatre in many parts of the world, especially ancient Greece and Japan, and used abstract scenery and dramatic lighting to create powerful moods. Playwrights such as Harold Pinter (b.1930) re-created shocking or depressing scenes from modern life on stage, as in this scene from his play *The Birthday Party*.

HARLEQUIN

Masked and dressed in a colourful diamond-patterned costume, Harlequin was the magical character in 18th and 19th century European fairground plays known as 'Harlequinades'.

◨ RUSSIAN FIRE-EATER

A performer breathes out clouds of fire in a dramatic display of skill in a Russian circus ring. Circuses are over 2000 years old. They began in ancient Roman times, with horrific gladiator fights, and continued in a smaller way, with animals, jugglers and acrobats, until around AD 1800. In the 19th century, Philip Astley in Britain and Barnum and Bailey in America re-created spectacular shows to entertain people. Modern circuses often feature high-tech effects, as well as traditional skills.

◨ MARIE LLOYD, MUSIC HALL STAR

Famous for her cheerful, witty and sometimes suggestive songs, Marie Lloyd (1870–1922) was the most famous star to entertain audiences in English music halls.

During the late 19th and early 20th centuries, music halls staged twice-nightly shows of about twenty different 'turns' or acts. These might include singing, dancing, conjuring, reciting monologues or telling jokes. Unusually for that time, many top performers were women, who earned high wages and had many fans.

Films and sound

MOST ideas about culture and civilization are passed from one generation to the next in words, music and visual images. These may be spoken, written or illustrated in books, or recorded and broadcast by modern media. Over the last two hundred years, new forms of communication have spread cultural ideas worldwide. Before 1900, new printing methods made magazines and newspapers cheap enough for ordinary people to buy. By the 1920s, radio, gramophones, movies, and recorded music provided entertainment for millions of people. After 1950, television became widespread, and today, the Internet brings new words and images to most parts of the world.

◪ MUTOSCOPE

Before the invention of films, people could watch moving pictures in a mutoscope. A sequence of images – each slightly different from the last – was mounted on cards inside a drum. When the viewer turned the handle, the images flicked over in rapid succession, giving the illusion of movement. Mutoscopes were a popular form of entertainment in amusement arcades, in about 1899. The most popular 'show' was called 'What the Butler Saw'.

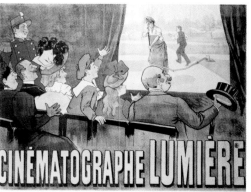

◪ MOVIE PIONEERS POSTER

This colourful poster is advertising the work of the French brothers Auguste and Louis Lumière, two of the world's most important cinema pioneers. In 1895 they invented the Cinématographe – a machine that combined a movie camera and film projector in one.

◳ GRAMOPHONE

The first-ever recorded sentence was 'Mary had a little lamb'. It was cut into a tinfoil cylinder and played on a phonograph, invented by Thomas Edison in 1877. Soon, record designers were able to improve the accuracy of recordings. By 1894, German-born Emile Berliner had designed the gramophone, a machine that played disc-shaped records of sung or spoken words. It amplified the sound through a bell-shaped horn.

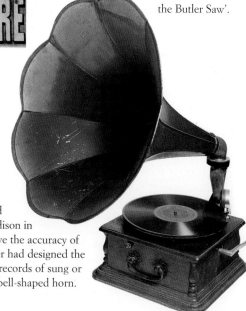

◨ SILENT MOVIE CAMERA

The first movies were silent. Large cameras were used to film the actors, who spoke their lines as if in a normal performance. On screen, their lip movements could be seen, but no spoken sounds were heard by the audience. In the cinema, a pianist or organist played live music to create the right mood for each scene. The first 'talkies' in which spoken words were heard, were made in the 1920s.

◨ MOVIE-STAR GLAMOUR

After about 1920, film stars such as Oscar-winning actress Audrey Hepburn (1929–93) attracted huge numbers of admirers. Although very well paid, movie stars had little privacy, and their lives were controlled by the movie makers.

◨ THE MUSIC INDUSTRY

Whitney Houston performs live at a Nelson Mandela benefit concert. Since beginning her singing career at the age of 11 in a gospel choir, Whitney has gone on to sell 75 million records in the United States alone, through Arista Records. The music industry developed rapidly during the 1950s, when the first long-playing vinyl records and hi-fi (high fidelity) gramophones were developed. About the same time, popular music shows were broadcast on TV, creating a vast audience for the latest sounds.

MICROPHONES

First invented in 1878, microphones are devices that convert sound energy into electrical energy. Modern microphones are small and lightweight, and are linked to amplifiers to increase the volume of sound in live performances.

Global village

DURING the 1960s, Canadian cultural historian Marshall McLuhan (1911–80) suggested that 20th-century electronic communications had turned the world into a 'global village'. He described how large amounts of information, flowing from one country to another, were destroying cultures. He also predicted that the ideas, beliefs, and values of wealthy superpowers, like the United States would overwhelm traditional lifestyles. By the year 2000, many people thought his predictions had come true.

◤ TEA PICKING IN JAPAN

Drinking tea is a strong cultural tradition in many parts of the world – notably Japan, China, India and Britain. In much of Asia, the people who grow and pick the tea are poor workers, while those who enjoy it are rich consumers. Since the 1980s, fair-trade organizations have campaigned to improve working conditions for producers, and to increase their pay.

◤ SOCCER

All over the world, children love playing and watching football. One of the favourite teams, as far apart as India and Africa, is Britain's Manchester United! Together, sport, and global communications have successfully united people from widely different cultures.

◤ FINANCIAL POWER

Billions of dollars change hands every day as brokers do deals in the world's financial markets, such as the Tokyo Stock Exchange. As they buy and sell shares in companies, dealers influence the financial future of countless people in foreign countries, raising or lowering food and fuel prices.

BACKPACKERS

Undeveloped countries are popular vacation destinations for backpackers from wealthy nations. Travel provides an exciting adventure and a chance to see and learn about other people's cultures firsthand. But the influence of foreign travellers' customs can undermine local traditions.

☑ THE POWER OF RADIO

Cheap transistor radios have revolutionized communications in many inaccessible regions, where there are no regular newspapers, and where hardly anyone can read. The radio brings the latest news from all over the world, as well as all kinds of entertainment, from dramas to soap operas.

◪ MULTINATIONAL BRANDS

Multinational corporations that produce popular brands of food and drink are always keen to find new buyers for their goods. Often the goods become status symbols for consumers in poorer countries, who choose them in preference to cheaper local brands. Some economists argue that the multinational brands harm the local economies by transferring money from poor countries to rich ones.

☑ INTERNET CAFÉ

The Internet began in 1969, when it was funded by the US Department of Defense. Military planners used the international computer network (the World Wide Web) to gather information. Today, the Internet is massive and constantly being updated. No single organization can control it. Users anywhere in the world who have access to a computer and telephone line – often through Internet cafés like this one in Singapore – can search for information or add their own views.

Glossary

AMPHITHEATRE
A circular or oval building with rows of seats which rise from an arena, where performances take place for an audience.

ANECDOTE
A short and often humorous narrative of an incident, usually involving real-life situations.

ARCHAEOLOGIST
An expert who finds out how people lived in the past by digging up and studying the places where they lived, and the remains they left behind.

ARCHITECT
A person who design buildings.

ART NOUVEAU
French phrase meaning 'new art', an elegant design style of natural flowing or swirling lines, fashionable at the beginning of the 20th century.

AUDITION
An interview to find suitable performers for roles in a play or musical performance. It usually involves candidates reading from a script, singing or giving a short performance, watched by the director.

BATON
A stick waved by the conductor of an orchestra to emphasise the rhythm and pattern of the music, so that everyone plays or sings the notes in the correct way at the correct time.

BIOGRAPHIES
Accounts of a person's life, written or told by someone else.

CERAMICS
Objects that are made by heating clay or similar materials, at high temperatures, so they become hard and brittle.

CHIAROSCURO
'Bright-dark', a painting or drawing technique which creates strong light-and-shadow effects using subtle colours.

CHIVALRY
Religious, moral and social rules of behaviour, which medieval knights were supposed to follow. Today it refers to polite, courteous behaviour, especially of men towards women.

CHOREOGRAPHER
The person who decides which dance steps and movements should be used by people during a ballet, musical or similar production, and then instructs and directs the performance of the dancers.

CHRONICLE
A continuous record of historical events, written in the order of time that they occurred, usually year by year.

CUBISM
A 20th century painting technique where the image is broken down into geometric

CUSTOM
A traditional practice, usually established by a particular community of people.

DIALOGUE
A conversation or discussion between two actors in a play or production, or between two representatives of groups with different ideas.

DICTATE
In one meaning, to give orders which others cannot question or refuse; powerful people called dictators do this. In another meaning, to speak or read aloud so that the words can be written down or recorded.

DRONE PIPES
The pipes within a set of bagpipes which play continuous, unchanging background sounds, as air is blown through them.

EPIC
A long story, poem, or tale, which tells of many great and magnificent deeds, especially involving a hero or heroine.

FOLK-TALE
A traditional story, based on fact or imagination, which is part of the history of a group of people, and which is passed down from generation to generation, usually by word of mouth

FRESCO
From the Italian word for 'fresh', a painting done on the plaster or render (coating) of a wall or ceiling using water-based paints, which are applied while the plaster is still wet.

GAMELAN
A traditional type of orchestra from the Indonesian islands of Java and Bali, with a wide range of instruments made mainly of the metal bronze.

GURU
A religious leader or teacher, who gives spiritual guidance and instruction.

HIEROGLYPHS
A system of writing which uses small pictures to represent words, syllables or sounds, and which was invented and used by the ancient Egyptians for their religious texts.

IMPASTO
A technique of applying oil or acrylic paint so thickly, with a brush or a palette knife, that the texture and thickness of the strokes remain in the paint.

IMPRESSIONISM
A technique developed by French artists in the 19th century, who painted very quickly outside, using very small dabs of paint to give an idea of the subject, rather than a detailed and realistic image.

LEGEND
A traditional story, which has come to be thought of as true, although there may be no facts to confirm that it is so.

MEDITATE
To think very deeply and intently, especially spiritually or religiously. People often sit in special positions or go to special places to meditate.

MORAL
Knowing the difference between right and wrong, good and bad, just and unjust, what is considered acceptable, and how to treat other people.

NEOCLASSICISM
A grand 19th century style of painting which tried to recreate the formal artistic glory or classical tradition of ancient Greece and Rome.

PANTOMIME
Originally a play performed using only actions, or mimes. Today a pantomime is usually a fairy story or folk tale made into a play with singing, dancing and spectacular costumes and scenery, often performed at Christmas.

PARABLE
A short religious story about everyday events, told to show examples of good and bad behaviour, and what can happen as a result

PILGRIMAGE
A journey made by a religious person to an important shrine or holy place, in order to pray or to worship.

PLECTRUM
A device for plucking the strings of a musical instrument, especially a guitar, such as a small triangular piece of plastic, held by hand.

PRODIGY
A person with unusual or exceptional talents, especially a child or young person who shows abilities which are far greater than usual for his or her age.

PROMPT
A person hidden from the audience just off-stage, who follows the script of a play or production, as the actors say their lines, and reminds or 'prompts' them if they forget what they have to say or do.

PROSE
The ordinary form of written language composed of phrases, sentences and paragraphs, rather than broken up into lines or verses, as in songs or poems.

RITUAL
A ceremony or event that is always carried out in the same way, according to strict rules, often for religious purposes.

SAGA
A medieval tale of Icelandic or Norwegian heroes and adventures. Modern-day sagas entail long and detailed stories about successive generations of the same family.

SATIRE
The use of techniques such as jokes, clever wit, irony or sarcasm, to expose wrong-doing or stupidity, or to make fun of an individual.

SCRIBE
A person who writes. Long ago, when few people could write and there was no printing, scribes copied out important documents and books.

SCRIPTURES
Sacred, solemn or authoritative pieces of writing, usually traditional and from ancient times. The collection of Christian literature known as the Bible is often called The Scriptures.

SHRINE
A religious place of worship, or the tomb of a holy person, such as a saint.

SUPERNATURAL
Forces, happenings or beings that cannot be explained by the laws of nature and science, and so are attributed to magic or the gods.

SYNCHRONIZED
When things happen at the same time or in a set pattern. For example, in films, the sound recording runs alongside the film so that the actors' words are heard precisely when their lips move – words and movements are 'in synch'.

THEORY
A set or system of ideas or proposals, which tries to explain how something works or happens. Theories are tested by observing and doing experiments, to find out if they are true.

TRADITION
The passing on of the culture of a group of people from old to young, including their customs, stories, history and beliefs.

TRAGEDY
A very sad event, such as an unhappy love affair, an appalling crime or a disaster. In theatre, the term refers to a play about a sequence of unhappy events which usually end for the worst.

ZOEPRAXISCOPE
A device that gives the illusion of a moving image, when a pictures on the inside of a spinning cylinder are viewed through slits in the cylinder.

Index

ACKNOWLEDGEMENTS

ART ARCHIVE Page 10 (t/r) Musée des Arts Décoratifs Paris/Dagli Orti, 13 (t/r) Archaeological Museum Filippi/Dagli Orti, 14 (t/r) Private Collection/Eileen Tweedy, (b/r) Art Archive, 16 (t/r) Victoria and Albert Museum London/Eileen Tweedy, 17 (c) Art Archive, 18 (t/r) Art Archive, 22 (t/r) The British Library, 23 (t/r) Musée du Château de Versailles/Dagli Orti, 24 (b/l) Civiche Racc d'Arte Moderna Pavia/Dagli Orti, 28 (t/r) Private Collection/Eileen Tweedy, (c/l) Courage Breweries/Eileen Tweedy Corbis: Page 18 (c/l) Bettmann, 25 (b) Archivo Iconografico, 27 (c) Robbie Jack, 34 (b/l) Historical Picture Archive, 35 (b/r) Hulton-Deutsch Collection, 37 (c/l) Charles E. Rotkin, (b) Joel W. Roger, 43 (t/r) National Library of Australia, 44 (c/l) Art Archive, 46 (t/r) Harper Collins Publishers, 47 (t/l) Art Archive, 48 (t/r) Victoria and Albert Museum London/Sally Chappell, (b/r) Art Archive, 49 (c/l) National Anthropological Museum Mexico/Dagli Orti, 51 (t/l) Dagli Orti, (c/l) National Anthropological Museum Mexico/Dagli Orti, (c/r) Musée des Arts Africains et Océaniens/ Dagli Orti, 56 (t/r) British Museum, 61 (t/l) United Society for Propagation of Gospel/Eileen Tweedy, 70 (b/l) Archaeological Museum Copan Honduras/Dagli Orti, 71 (t/l) Museo Larco Herrera Lima/Album/J. Enrique Molina, 75 (t/r) Dagli Orti, 76 (c/l) British Museum, 78 (b/l) San Domenico Maggiore Naples/Dagli Orti, 79 (c) San Domenico Maggiore Naples/Dagli Orti, 81 (t/r) Francesco Venturi, 82 (t/r) Art Archive, 84 (t/r) British Museum/Dagli Orti, (c/l) Museum der Stadt Wien/Dagli Orti, 86 (t/r) British Library, (c/l) Museo Correr Venice/Dagli Orti, 87 (t/l) Museo Bibliografico Musicale Bologna/Dagli Orti, 88 (t/r) Society Friends Music Vienna/Dagli Orti, 89 (t/l) Royal Ballet Benevolent Fund/Eileen Tweedy, (t/r) Museo Bibliografico Musicale Bologna/Dagli Orti, (b/r) Conservatoire Prague/Dagli Orti, 94 (t/r) San Pietro Maiella Conservatoire Naples/Dagli Orti, Page 100 (c/l) Musée du Louvre Paris/Dagli Orti, 101 (t/r) Red-Head, 102 (t/r) Museo Civico Udine/Dagli Orti, (c/l) British Museum/Eileen Tweedy, 103 (c/l) British Museum/Eileen Tweedy, (c/r) Art Archive, 105 (t/r) Musée des Arts Décoratifs Paris/Dagli Orti, 108 (c/l) Bibliothèque des Arts Décoratifs Paris/Dagli Orti, 112 (t/c) Dagli Orti, 113 (c/r) Dagli Orti, 114 (t/r) Dagli Orti, 116 (t/r) Historical Museum Armenia Erevan/Dagli Orti, (c/l) Egyptian Museum Cairo/Dagli Orti, (b/r) Galleria d'Arte Moderna Rome/Dagli Orti, 119 (c/r) Art Archive, 122 (c/l) Museo Correr Venice/Dagli Orti, 126 (c/l) Mireille Vautier, 130 (t/r) Etruscan Necropolis Tarquinia/Dagli Orti, (c) Eileen Tweedy, 131 (t/r) Galleria d'Arte Moderna Udine Italy/Dagli Orti, 134 (c/l) Musée Bonnat Bayonne France/Dagli Orti, 135 (t/l) Art Archive, 140 (t/r) Francesco Venturi, 142 (t/r) Richard Wagner Museum Bayreuth/Dagli Orti, 146 (c/l) Victoria and Albert Museum, London/Eileen Tweedy, 160 (t/r) Archaeological Museum Naples/Dagli Orti, (c/l) Musée Condé Chantilly/Dagli Orti, 161 (t/l) British Museum/Eileen Tweedy, (t/r) Wheelwright Museum, (b/l) Mireille Vautier, 163 (t/l) British Library, (t/r) Musée des Antiquités St Germain en Laye/Dagli Orti, 164 (b/r) Museo Larco Herrera Lima/Album/J. Enrique Molina, 165 (t/r) Victoria and Albert Museum London/Eileen Tweedy, 166 (t/r) Musée Condé Chantilly / Dagli Orti, 167 (b/l) Tate Gallery London/Eileen Tweedy, 168 (b/r) Antochiw Collection Mexico/Mireille Vautier, 170 (b/r) Dagli Orti, 171 (c/l) Musée du Château de Versailles/Dagli Orti, (b/r) Domenica del Corriere/Dagli Orti, 172 (t/r) National Gallery Budapest/Dagli Orti, (c/l) Biblioteca Nazionale Marciana Venice/Dagli Orti, 173 (t/l) San Francesco Assisi/Dagli Orti, (b/r) British Library, 174 (b/r) Villa of the Mysteries Pompeii/Dagli Orti, 175 (t/l) Art Archive, 176 (t/r) Museo teatrale alla Scala Milan/Dagli Orti, 177 (t/l) Richard Wagner Museum Bayreuth/Dagli Orti, (b/r) Oldsaksammlung Oslo/Dagli Orti, 178 (b/l) Neuschwanstein Castle Germany/Dagli Orti, (b/r) Bardo Museum Tunis, 179 (t/l) Archaeological Museum Naples/Dagli Orti, (b/l) Palazzo Arco Mantua Italy/Dagli Orti, 180 (t/r) Museo Civico Vicenza/Dagli Orti, (b/r) Nicolas Sapieha, 181 (c/l) Art Archive, 184 (t/r) Richard Wagner Museum Bayreuth/Dagli Orti, (c/l) Dagli Orti, 185 (c/l) British Library, 191 (t/l) Dagli Orti, (b) Dagli Orti, 192 (b/l) Lucien Bitlon Collection Paris/Dagli Orti, 193 (t/l) Scrovegni Chapel Padua/Dagli Orti, (c/r) Art Archive, 194 (t/r) Santa Maria dlla Scala Hospital Siena/Dagli Orti, (c/l) Museo Correr Venice/Dagli Orti, (b) Museo del Prado Madrid/Art Archive, 195 (t/l) Galleria degli Uffizi Florence/Dagli Orti, (c/r) Galleria Brera Milan/Album/Joseph Martin, (b) Windsor Castle/Art Archive, 196 (t/r) Musée du Louvre Paris/Jaqueline Hyde, (c/l) Malmaison Musée du Chateau/Dagli Orti, (b/r) Musée de Beaux Arts Nantes/Dagli Orti, 197 (c/l) Musée du Louvre Paris/Dagli Orti, (b/r) Gulbenkian Foundation Lisbon/Dagli Orti, 198 (t/r) Musée d'Orsay Paris/Dagli Orti, (c/l) Musée du Louvre Paris/Dagli Orti, (b/r) Musée d'Orsay Paris/Dagli Orti, 199 (t/r) Metropolitan Museum of Art New York/Album/Joseph Martin, (c/l) Jean Walter & Paul Guillaume Coll/Dagli Orti, (b/r) Musée Sorolla Madrid/Album/Joseph Martin, 200 (b/r) Moderna Museet Stockholm/Dagli Orti, 201 (c/l) Konstant Parmeke Mus Jabbeke/Dagli Orti, 202 (t/r) Torre Aquila Trento/Dagli Orti, (c/l) Musée d'Orsay Paris/Dagli Orti, 203 (t/r) Victoria and Albert Museum London/Sally Chappell, 204 (c/l) Victoria and Albert Museum London/Sally Chappell, (b/r) Museum der Stadt Wien/Dagli Orti, 205 (b/l) Eileen Tweedy, 206 (t/l) Musée du Louvre Paris/Dagli Orti, (b) Museo Capitolino Rome/Dagli Orti, 207 (t/l) Dagli Orti, 208 (t/r) Musée d'Orsay Paris/Dagli Orti, (c/l) Museo del Oro Lima/Dagli Orti, (b/r) Middelheim Sculpture Garden Holland/Nicolas Sapieha, 209 (c/l) Dagli Orti, (b/r) Art Archive, 210 (b/r) Sao Paulo Art Museum Brazil/Dagli Orti, 211 (t/l) Victoria and Albert Museum London/Sally Chappell, 212 (t/r) Art Archive, (b) Dagli Orti, 213 (t/l) Private Collection/Dagli Orti, (c/l) Dagli Orti, (r) Victoria and Albert Museum London/Sally Chappell, 214 (t/r) Eileen Tweedy, (l) Eileen Tweedy, (b) Lords Gallery/Dagli Orti, 215 (t/r) Victoria and Albert Museum London/Eileen Tweedy, (c/l) Musée de l'Affiche Paris/Dagli Orti, 216 (c/l) Galleria della Uffizi Florence/Dagli Orti, 217 (t/r) Musée du Louvre Paris/Dagli Orti, 224 (t/r) British Library, (r) Archaeological Museum Lima/Dagli Orti, (c) Eileen Tweedy, 225 (t/l) Real biblioteca de lo Escorial/Dagli Orti, (t/r) Private Collection Paris/Dagli Orti, 226 (c) Victoria and Albert Museum London/Eileen Tweedy, 227 (b) Chester Brummel, 230 (t/r) Musée des Arts Décoratifs Paris/Dagli Orti, 232 (c/l) British Library/Eileen Tweedy, 236 (t/r) Art Archive, 237 (t/l) Osterreichisches National Bibliothek Vienna/Harper Collins Publishers, 238 (t/r) Musée du Château de Versailles/Dagli Orti, 239 (t/r) Album/Joseph Martin, 240 (t/r) Dagli Orti, (b/l) Edward Grieg House, Nordas Lake/Dagli Orti, 241 (t/l) British Library, 242 (t/l) British Museum/Eileen Tweedy, 243 (c/l) Museum der Stadt Wien/Dagli Orti, 244 (c/l) Musée de l'Affiche Paris/Dagli Orti, 245 (t/r) Art Archive **CORBIS:** Page 43 (c/r) Alison Wright, 47 (b/l) Paul Almasy, 53 (b/r) Lindsay Hebberd, 54 (c) Dean Conger, 57 (t/l) Lawrence Manning, 59 (b) Richard T. Nowitz, 61 (c) Daniel Lainé, (c/l) Jerry Cooke, 63 (t/r) Corbis, 64 (b) Adam Wolfitt, 67 (t) The Purcell Team, 73 (t/l) Christine Osborne, (c/r) Lynn Goldsmith, (b/r) Charles & Josette Lenars, 76 (b) Sergio Dorantes, 77 (b) Michael S. Yamashita, (b) Michael S. Yamashita, 80 (c/l) Bettmann, (b) Wolfgang Kaehler, 82 (t/l) Neal Preston, (b/r) Reuters New Media Inc, 83 (t/l) Reuters New Media Inc, (t/r) Neal Preston, (b/r) Kevin Fleming, 85 (t/r) Dean Conger, (b) Gunter Marx Photography, 87 (b) Roger Ressmeyer, 88 (b/r) Jonathan Blair, 89 (b/l) Mitchell Gerber, 90 (b/l) Mosaic Images, 91 (t/l) Bettmann, (c/r) S.I.N., 93 (b/l) Neal Preston, 94 (b/r) Michael Pole, 95 (b) Duomo, 96 (c/l) Neal Preston, 97 (t/r) Chris Lisle, 115 (t/r) Mitchell Gerber, (b) Lindsay Hebberd, 135 (c/l) Hulton-Deutsch Collection, 137 (c/r) Robbie Jack, 138 (t/r) Hulton-Deutsch Collection, (b) Ira Nowinski, 141 (t/l) Hulton-Deutsch Collection, 142 (b) Robbie Jack (cont'd page 143), 144 (c/l) Penny Tweedie, (b) Gunter Marx, 147 (b) Robbie Jack, 150 (t/r) Hulton-Deutsch Collection, 151 (b) Bettmann, 157 (t/r) Stephanie Maze, 170 (b/l) Historical Picture Archive, 187 (b) Peter Tumley, 210 (t/r) Hulton-Deutsch Collection, 211 (b) Genevieve Naylor, (b/l) Bettmann, 217 (b/r) Robert Holmes, Page 220 (c/l) David & Peter Turnley, 221 (t/l) Staffan Widstrand, (b/l) Hulton-Deutsch Collection, 228 (t/r) Michael S. Yamashita, 229 (b) Macduff Everton, 233 (c/r) David & Peter Tumley, 235 (t/r) Bob Krist, (b) Dave Bartruff, 237 (b) Steve Chenn, 239 (c/l) Stephanie Maze, (b) Stephanie Maze, 241 (c) Catherine Kamow, 242 (b) Michael S. Yamashita, 243 (t/r) Hulton-Deutsch Collection, (b) Jeffrey L.Rotman, 245 (b/r) Corbis, 246 (c) David & Peter Tumley, 247 (t/l) Danny Lehman, (b) Macduff Everton **KOBAL:** Page 19 (t/r) Selznik Films, 20 (b) Paramount, 21 (t/r) EON / United Artists, 26 (b/l) UFA, 27 (t/r) Sparham, Laurie/Miramax Films/Universal Pictures, 31 (t/r) MGM, (b/r) Kobal Collection, 32 (t/r) Paramount, (c/l) 20th Century Fox, (b/r) Kobal Collection, 33 (c) MGM, (b/l) Umbrella/Rosenblum/Virgin Films, 35 (t/l) Distant Horizons/Miramax, (c/r) 20th Century Fox, 95 (c/l) Kobal Collection, (c/r) Kobal Collection, Page 123 (t/r) Warner Bros, Page 136 (b) Kobal Collection, 137 (t/r) Kobal Collection, (b/l) Kobal Collection, 139 (t/l) Kobal Collection, (t/r) Columbia, (b/r) EMI/MGM, 143 (t/l) Magna Theatres, (b/l) Aceent/RAI, (c/r) Konow Rolph/Mandalay, 146 (b/r) Rank, 148 (t/r) Kobal Collection, 149 (t/r) Warner Bros, (b/r) Jim Henson Productions, 151 (t/r) Edison, 152 (t/r) Kobal Collection, (c/l) Kobal Collection, (b) Tursi, Mario/20th Century Fox, (b/r) Kobal Collection, 153 (c/l) Kobal Collection, (r) Kobal Collection, 154 (c/l) 20th Century Fox, (b) Warner Bros, 155 (c) United Artists, 155 (b) Columbia, 156 (b) Joey Delvalle, 174 (c/r) Walt Disney, 176 (b) Kobal Collection, 186 (t/r) Kobal Collection, (b/r) Warner Bros, 187 (c/r) Ken Regan/Columbia, 220 (b) Disney, 225 (c/l) MGM, (b) Lucas Film/20th Century Fox, 244 (t/r) Kobal Collection, 245 (r) Paramount

The publishers would like to thank Anne Frank Stichting of the Anne Frank House for the use of photographic material.

All other photographs are from: MKP Archives; Corel; PhotoDisc